TWO CENTURIES OF CHANGE

The History of a Wharfedale Parish,
St. Mary BV, Burley-in-Wharfedale

Margaret and Dennis Warwick
Foreword by Reverend Michael Burley

BURLEY-IN-WHARFEDALE
LOCAL HISTORY GROUP
PUBLICATIONS
ON BEHALF OF
ST MARY'S PAROCHIAL CHURCH COUNCIL
2009

First published in 2009

Burley-in-Wharfedale Local History Group Publications
On behalf of St. Mary's Parochial Church Council

Pages formatted on Microsoft ® Publisher
Printed by City Graphics Ltd., Bradford, BD8 0LH.

British Library Cataloguing in Publication Data
A catalogue record for this book is available from the British Library

ISBN 978-0-9524291-4-2

CONTENTS

FOREWORD

Shortly after I arrived in Burley in Wharfedale I was asked to select a piece of church furniture to commemorate the lives of Pip and Jay Hayes, much loved members of the St. Mary's family. The P.C.C. and I decided to commission a Vicars' Board from Thompsons the 'mousemen'. (For those interested in trivia the board took a long time to arrive as the original board was carved with Wharfedale spelt Wharfdale!) The Vicars' board at St. Mary's lists the names of those who have served as incumbents of this parish. The board is a historical record, but more importantly it helps us to connect, as part of the 'communion of saints', with those who have served here through the centuries.

Dennis and Margaret Warwick have used the names and dates on the board as a basis for their historical account of St. Mary's. Some of the Vicars have well documented lives, some less so; some served in parishioners' living memory and some come from a very different culture and life experience. Reading through the accounts of ministries in Burley I have been struck by how similar our problems and opportunities are. Money, or lack of it, is a constant problem for the church. The changing nature of the community of Burley in Wharfedale is reflected, and how issues facing the national church affect our communal life.

I often look at the names on the Vicar's board and remember that no matter how long I serve, I hold stewardship of this Church for a very small period in God's great scheme of things. All of us on the Vicars' board would agree that the Jesus we worship is still the same yesterday, today and forever and the good news of His love is an inspiration in the past, in the present and into the future. It is in His service and to the honour and glory of God that this history of our church in Burley in Wharfedale is offered. Recording the history of St. Mary's has involved much research and I am grateful to Dennis and Margaret for undertaking this. I commend the Warwicks' readable account of this Parish Church to you.

With every blessing,   Michael Burley (Vicar).

5

PREFACE AND ACKNOWLEDGEMENTS

For our little world is only to be converted to Christ as the great world outside it. The nearer we come to fulfilling the idea now, and here, "one fold under one shepherd" the nearer shall we attain to Christ.

Rev. Dr. Black, 1864.

Our intention is to provide as thorough a history of our Church and Parish as is possible from the available records. We are indebted to two histories, those of David Nealy, *The Parish Church of Burley-in-Wharfedale,* 1960, and of Frank Newbould, *A Short History of the Parish Church of St. Mary the Blessed Virgin,* 1993. Both of these call upon detail from Rev. Dr. Black, Vicar of Burley until 1896, who kept copious records of his forty one years in the Parish and put many of these in a bound volume, entitled *Historical Memorials of Burley-By-The-Wharfe,* which dates from about 1880. The *Historical Memorials* has recently been rebound and it is evident that his scholarly mind was constantly relating his contemporary experience of the Parish to its historical and ecclesiastical context

We have consulted other sources, such as H. Speight, *Lower Wharfedale,* 1900, but he too seems to have drawn mainly on Dr. Black's papers. Rev R.V. Taylor, *Ecclesiae Leodienses or Architectural Sketches of the Churches of Leeds and Neighbourhood,* 1875, contains a chapter on Burley Church in Wharfedale, with a little historical information. Primary sources include records formerly kept in the Vestry at St. Mary's, and now held in the Bradford Central Library, by West Yorkshire Archives Service. For instance the *Town Book* contains the accounts of the principal officers of Burley Township from the mid eighteenth century to the first decades of the nineteenth. Among them are the records of the Chapel Warden. He was responsible for maintaining the old Burley Chapel of Ease as a public building, on behalf of the rate payers of Burley and the Church Wardens of Otley, in whose parish the Chapel lay. A brief history is also contained among the Horsfall Papers in the West Yorkshire Archives in Bradford. A

Copy Book, origin unknown, contains in fine copperplate script, a plan of the old Chapel, and copies of deeds and letters concerning the appointment and remuneration of a minister and the ownership and rents of pews. The entries date from 1645 to 1835 and in one or two places are initialled EFM or possibly EJM. No clue is given as to the authorship. Could it have been a young member of the Maude family who lived at Burley House until the nineteenth century?

A report carried in the *Leeds Intelligencer* of 24th June 1843, describes the consecration of St. Mary's by the then Lord Bishop of Ripon. The Faculty for the replacement of the old Chapel and the construction of St. Mary's is kept in the York Diocesan records at the Borthwick Institute at York University. From this time Burley was regarded as having a Church rather than a Chapel. St. Mary's became a Parish Church in 1856, when Burley and Menston were separated from the Parish of Otley. The *Vestry Book*, contains records of Vestry Meetings held in Burley from 1865 to 1922, though there are also appended other papers dating from before 1865 and after 1922. Principally it contains the appointments of Church Wardens and financial statements of income and expenditure by the Church. Dr. Black's handwriting figures prominently in the *Vestry Book* until his death in 1896. The Lord Bishop of Ripon, Charles Thomas Longley (later Archbishop of Canterbury) kept notebooks recording visitations to the many parishes in his Diocese. The entries for Burley list seven visits from 1837 to 1856. The notebooks are to be found in the Special Collections of the Brotherton Library, Leeds University (and we thank Gordon Forster for pointing us to them). The Bishop noted names of the incumbents, the condition of the Chapel, its rebuilding, church attendance, services held, numbers in the congregation, the frequency of communion, Day and Sunday School attendances and how frequently catechising occurred. The records of the Ripon Diocese reside in the Leeds Archives at Sheepscar, where we were able to examine the faculty and all the correspondence related to it, which was obtained for the extension of the Chancel at St. Mary's in 1869. Details of the succession of Clergy who served St. Mary's from the 1850s have been obtained from the collection of Crockfords Clerical Directories, held at the Borthwick Institute, York University and at the Information

Other primary sources should be mentioned. Through the generosity of Veronica Rowe of County Dublin, a descendant of Florence Arnold-Forster (O'Brien after her marriage to Robin O'Brien an Irish solicitor), the hand written journals of Florence's sister Frances have been deposited in the Brotherton Library, the University of Leeds. These cover the years from 1871 to 1887, and though her family led a very peripatetic life, the place she called "home" was Wharfeside in Burley-in-Wharfedale. There are many references to Church services and descriptions of her work as a Bible Class teacher at St. Mary's. More recently, Veronica has been transcribing the diaries of Florence, and these are adding some further information about Burley and St. Mary's in the period from 1870 until the turn of the century. Much of the correspondence of Jane Martha Forster, wife of W.E. Forster, millowner in Burley and M.P. for Bradford from 1861 to 1886, the adoptive parents of Frances and Florence, also refers to events at St. Mary's. She lived at Wharfeside from 1852 to 1899, and most of her letters are archived in Trinity College, Dublin, many of which we have read there. Another source is the handwritten journal of John Lupton, a retired butcher and Sidesman and Clerk to St. Mary's Church at the beginning of the twentieth century. This provides some information about the Church at that time. Unfortunately only fragments of the original diary remain. Local newspapers, the *Wharfedale and Airedale Observer*, the *Ilkley Gazette* and the *Bradford Telegraph and Argus*, have provided news items, pictures and comments on events and people.

For the twentieth and twenty first centuries, we have consulted Parish Magazines, though only a few of the many early ones which were printed remain. The minutes of the Parochial Church Council, and those of Annual Vestry and Parochial meetings from 1920 up to the present decade have survived more or less intact. For the first half of the twentieth century, it was fortunate that they were kept by head teachers of the National school, who seem to have acquired the office of secretary to the PCC as a matter of course. We have consulted those incumbents who have not yet left this earthly life or who remain accessible to us. Rev John Beardsmore, Vicar from 1957 to 1969, Rev John Tidy, Vicar from 1983 to 1992 and Rev Peter Sutcliffe, Vicar from 1993 to 2003, have been helpful. We have drawn on our own memories and those of older members of the present congregation along with Churchwardens, past and present. To the present incumbent, Rev Michael Burley, we owe much gratitude for his forbearance of our sometimes intrusive requests for information as well as to his research into the life of Dr. Black. We are also grateful to Rev Eileen McLean, Rev James Turnbull, and Rev Canon Malcolm Emmel. Many of our fellow and former parishioners have offered advice too when our memory has failed us. Some have provided documents and photographs to help in our research. Especially we would like to thank Chris Aldred, Jason Atkinson, Sylvia Baty, Peter and Kath Bennett, Gail Boole, Anne Clough, Nigel and Jennifer Cottam, Keith and Mary Dale, John and Jan Dibb, Glynne and Yvonne Edwards, Paul and Gill Evans, Enid Feather, Jane Gurung, Gerald Hodges, Michael Hodges, John Horton, Kelvin and Nancy Newberry, Joan Lewis Ogden, Frank and Barbara Schofield, Mark Selby, David and Pam Sowman, Janet Squire, Bert and Judy Taylor, Ian and Hilary Walsh, David and Philip Warwick, Duncan Watts, Fay Wise, Arthur Woodhead. In the early part of our research we consulted Raymond Gill, whose death in 2009 deprived us of a memory of Church and Church people that is irreplaceable. As ever we thank Sally Gunton whose collection of old postcards of Burley has provided several additions to our illustrations. Wherever possible we have acknowledged the ownership of the photographs used as illustrations. Most of the unacknowledged were taken by the authors.

In writing this history we want to give a sense of change but also of how much continuity there has been in the church, its services and its teaching. We must at the same time acknowledge the influence of economic, social, cultural and religious changes in Britain and the World. Inevitably there are many shortcomings in our account. Documentation is very patchy and memories are liable to error. As a result some aspects of Church life have had more emphasis than others but we have tried to be faithful to the tenets of historical research.

CHAPTER ONE

INTRODUCTION

The Wharfe or <u>Swift</u> River, about fifty miles in length, rises in the southeast of Cam Fell, and passing Aughtershaw and fourteen other villages, reaches Bolton, and then winds past St.Peter's Addingham; All Saints, Ilkley; All Hallows, Weston and St. Mary the Virgin, Burley.

Rev. Dr. Black, 1868.

The older Churches of Wharfedale tend to be near the river, and several like St. Mary's stand above it, perhaps on ancient religious sites. An observer in 1875 noted that St. Mary's 'is ...a striking object to the traveller from Otley to Ilkley and Skipton, as it stands upon the highest plot of ground in the vicinity of Burley Hall'[1].

Towards the end of Dr. Black's volume is a printed paper[2] in which he gives his account of the history of the two villages and their religious establishments. He indicates that the records of Burley are very sketchy indeed.

1. St Mary's spire, Burley Hall and the River Wharfe.

There is since his time hearsay evidence of pre-Roman age settlement. In the 1950s excavation for a car lift at a garage on Main Street a hammer of Iron Age type was dug out. It is very probable as Black points out that there was a small fortification here in Roman times, guarding the Roman road to Ilkley. The derivation of the place name Burley or Burghelai as it was in the Domesday Book of 1087, suggests a fortification (*Burgh*) of some kind. All traces have gone, but Burley was a small hamlet in the

Wharfe Valley in Saxon times, and part of the old Parish of Otley, whose Church dates from the 7th Century. The parish of Otley was very large and its record in the Domesday Book Survey of 1087 indicates that it was in the possession of the Archbishop of York. Burley came to have a small chapel, possibly as early as the twelfth century. There is no certainty about this date, or its dedication, which Black suggests was to St. Mary the Virgin, but by 1632, he claims, this chapel was in ruins.

About that time, the leading landowners in Burley, Stead, Menston, Weston and Denton came together to 're-edify the Chapel of Burley'. Amongst them the Vavasours, Fairfaxes, Maudes, Steads, Jenkinsons, Hartleys and Pulleyns assigned land and endowments for a new chapel to be built and a minister appointed. Deeds dated 1645 indicate that a Chapel was built to accommodate 160, with pews allocated to the leading families and a small space at the rear for others. The pew rents amounted to something less than £30 per year, which provided income for the maintenance of the ministry. There were also gifts of land and the income from these amounted to about £16 per year. £4 per year was donated by the Vavasour family. Taylor in his account of Burley's Church, notes that 'the old Chapel [was] built by the Fairfax family, in consequence of

2.

THE OLD CHAPEL
About 1640

Photograph of Oil Painting of the Old Chapel, painted by W. L. Dobson.

the road to the Parish Church at Otley being often flooded'[3]. It was a simple structure, which came to be known as the Fairfax Chapel, and was like the small Chapel alongside the main road through Bramhope. A house for the Minister was also provided in the Church yard.

Some two hundred years later this Chapel was 'not in good repair'[4] and had insufficient accommodation for the growing population of the village. Prominent inhabitants of Burley and Otley petitioned the Diocese of Ripon for permission to demolish the old building and erect a new enlarged Church on the same site. The old Chapel had only seating for 160 persons, 130 of which were privately rented, whereas the new building was to have 507 sittings of which 259 were free[5]. Some of the windows in the new building are dedicated to the memory of the early founders. There is also a tablet on the west wall which originally had been in the old chapel. It was taken to Burley Hall during the rebuilding. and later found in the stables there by Dr. Black.

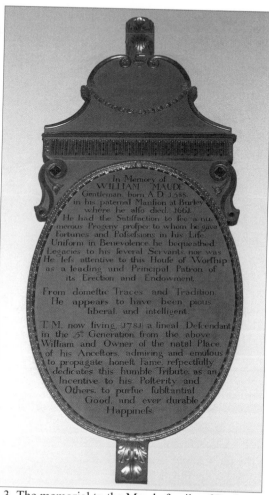

3. The memorial to the Maude family of Burley House.

This Chapel was the only public building in Burley and its Vestry was indeed the seat of local government under the Poor Law Act of 1601. Along with welfare for the poor, the Law required that the village Chapel and roads should be maintained and, as far as possible, crime prevented. The principal inhabitants were made responsible for all of these tasks. The offices of Chapel Warden, Surveyor and Constable, as well as Overseer, circulated annually among them. The amount of work involved varied, the duties of the Overseers probably being the most time consuming. Much depended on the efficiency of these voluntary officers for the smooth running of the community.

The Chapel Warden was responsible for the upkeep of the Chapel building, paying dues to Otley Parish Church (always the largest annual payment) and various other public tasks, such as having mad dogs and polecats killed. There was a Parish Clerk who received an annual income paid out of the Poor Rate. In the 1770s the Rate was assessed at 3 pence in the pound. According to the accounts of Michael Stead, Chapel Warden in 1772, the Poor Rate allocated for the upkeep of the Chapel equalled £12 12s. 6d. Otley Parish Church received 80 percent of that amount. Small sums were allocated for cleaning and repairing windows, whitening the Chapel walls and cleaning out the Chapel[6]. These accounts were separate from those kept by the incumbent for his duties in the Township of Burley.

The upkeep of the Chapel was not sufficient to prevent the whole structure deteriorating to the point where serious problems were apparent. As we have noted, in 1841 it was decided to have the Chapel replaced by a superior building which could house a growing congregation. Meanwhile other events had taken place which probably helped to hasten that decision.

In 1835 cooperation between non-resident incumbent of Burley, Rev. E. Hodgkinson and John Peele Clapham[7] then living at Burley Hall, led to the formation of an ecumenical village Sunday School. Clapham had looked with some dismay on the poor state, as he saw it, not only of the Hall which he rented, but also the Fairfax chapel adjacent to it. No effort was being made to instruct the children at the east end of the village, and

though
> *our brethren the Wesleyans had been long at work in the village*
> *and had done good service in partially supplying the deficien-*
> *cies of the Establishment; at least one half of the children of this*
> *populous district ran wild in the lanes and fields, 'no man' ap-*
> *parently 'caring for their souls'*[8].

Clapham thought Hodgkinson, the new curate, to be "of more earnest spirit", and sought his support in starting a Sunday School. Though there were differences in religious opinions, which caused Clapham some doubts about the project, a decision was reached to start a 'Village Sunday School' with the support of all Anglicans, Wesleyans, Independents and Baptists present. An executive committee representative of these groups was set up. Classes were first held in an empty cottage, which was too small for the numbers attending. They then moved into the old Fairfax Chapel but protests from the congregation there, led to Clapham building the three cottages to the right of Post Office Yard, making their upper rooms available for classes.

Rules had been agreed at a public meeting in April 1835 which stated that the school was intended for the benefit of all children over 5 years whatever their parents' religious denomination. The teaching was to be based on the Old and New Testaments, and the principles of Christianity, avoiding "the peculiar tenets of any denomination". A year later, as they were about to move into the newly built school rooms, a public meeting was called by the Committee, and a progress report was given. The school was said to have 104 scholars and 42 teachers. In addition to the Sunday classes there were evening classes for Bible study, reading and writing. The report concludes
> *..though the sky has not been always clear, nor the path always*
> *smooth, we have much reason for thankfulness, that our present*
> *prospects are peculiarly encouraging*[9].

The ecumenical experiment, however, continued only for a short time. Through the influence of Mrs Lydia Anderton, of Burley House, a new resident curate was appointed to Burley. This young man, Rev. W.G.

Wilkinson, at first accepted the existing arrangements with Clapham and the Committee, but then began to introduce the teachers and scholars to the idea of having a separate Anglican school. He seems to have persuaded some, perhaps even threatening them with loss of employment, to join his enterprise and Clapham sadly saw his erstwhile worries fulfilled. He wrote in *The Annals*:

> *Lamentable proof was given that sinister influences, supporting the resident Curate, were stronger than all the good intentions and efforts of the non-resident Incumbent[10].*

Clapham moved out of the Hall, and built the Grange as his private residence and Salem Chapel and Sunday School near the junction of Town Street (now Main Street) and Moor Lane (the present Station Road) in 1840.

The Anglicans went ahead with a scheme to have a National School, with the financial support of Mrs Anderton, and this opened on Back Lane in 1837. It was built on land given by William Fairbank of Otley and functioned both as Day and a Sunday School. It was this school that helped to make the demolition of the old Chapel feasible as it was licensed for religious services from 1841 until the new Church was completed.

The foundation stone for St. Mary's was laid on 14th October 1841 and, less than two years later on Monday 18th June 1843, the Church was consecrated in a service led by the Lord Bishop of Ripon, Charles Thomas Longley. The proceedings were described in detail in the *Leeds Intelligencer* of 24th June. (See Appendix Two)

The Church was described as being in the Early English style of architecture with a lantern and spire. The architect was Walker Rawstorne of Bradford. It was 92 feet long and 34 feet wide. The east end had three lancet stained glass windows by William Wailes of Newcastle. Other windows would appear to have been in clear glass at this time. The interior was relatively plain, with box pews and a spacious gallery at the west end.

DONATIONS

IN AID OF THE ERECTION OF

The Church of S. Mary the Virgin,

BURLEY-IN-WHARFEDALE.—1842-43.

	£ s. d.	£ s. d.
Her Majesty the Queen Dowager		20 0 0
The Ripon Diocesan Society		300 0 0
The Incorporated Society		150 0 0
Messrs. Greenwood and Whitaker		100 0 0
" " " (Second Donation)		50 0 0
Mrs. Anderton		50 0 0
" " (Second Donation)		50 0 0
E. J. Mitchell, Esq., Bradford, collected from Members of the Christian Knowledge Society		375 13 6½
The Rev. J. A. Rhodes		30 0 0
His Grace the Archbishop of York		25 0 0
Co-operative Society		29 7 0
Miss Hartley		20 0 0
W. J. Maude, Esq.		20 0 0
Mrs. Lawrence, Studley Park		10 0 0
Benjamin Thomson, Esq.		10 0 0
J. P. Clapham, Esq.		10 0 0
William Fairbank, Esq.		10 0 0
Mr. Joseph Whitehead		10 0 0
Mr. Francis Foster		10 0 0
Mrs. Leah, Bierley Hall		10 0 0
Misses Harrison, Sheffield		10 0 0
Mr. William Booth, Leeds		10 0 0
Mrs. Hargreaves		10 0 0
Rev. E. Hodgkinson		5 5 0
Mr. Stephen Fawcet		5 5 0
Mr. Thos. Wade		5 0 0
Mr. Hartley, Otley		5 0 0
Mr. Robert Walsh, Halifax		5 0 0
Mr. Wilks, Burley		5 0 0
F. Billam, Esq., Otley		5 0 0
J. B. Hyndman, Esq., London		5 0 0
W. Gray, Esq., York		5 0 0
George Leather, Esq., Leeds	5 0 0	
J. W. Leather, Esq.	5 0 0	
Thos. Cadman, Esq.	5 0 0	
Mr. T. Brown	3 0 0	
Mr. Edward Brown, Keighley	5 0 0	
Mr. Thos. Brown, jun., Manchester	5 0 0	28 0 0
		£1,393 10 6½

4. List of donors in 1842, showing Royal and Archepiscopal support for the appeal. Local donors include the mill owners Greenwood and Whitaker, Mrs Anderton of Burley Lodge and John Peele Clapham of the Grange and Salem.

It was said to have seating for just over 500 people. The cost of the building was estimated to have been £1774. The Diocese of Ripon had contributed £300; the Incorporated Society for Building Churches, £150; and general subscriptions, £989. Local inhabitants had provided materials and labour to the amount of almost £44. The land on which the Church was built and its surrounds including the burial ground covered 1700 square yards (1421 m^2). The work was supervised by a local building committee, including Jonas Whitaker (millowner), William Fairbank and Edward J. Mitchell. In his report of visitations to the Church after its consecration, Bishop Longley notes that the congregation a year after was 150 in the morning and 250 in the afternoon. There were monthly communion services with an average of 16 attending. The morning and afternoon congregations in 1847, 1850 and 1853 were much the same as in the earlier year, but he infers that there had been a gradual increase in the number of communicants at the eucharist[11].

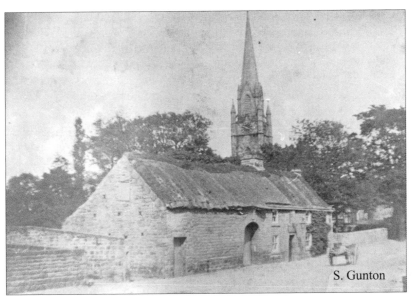

S. Gunton

5. The new Church spire and the thatched roof Malt Shovel inn.

Rev Edmund Hodgkinson became the Perpetual Curate in Burley in 1835 while also being the Perpetual Curate in Baildon, also part of the parish of Otley. He remained at St. Mary's until 1848. Hodgkinson initiated the celebration of the holy eucharist in the old Chapel, bringing vessels for the administration from Baildon. Bishop Longley in his notes of visitations in 1837, notes that the eucharist was celebrated about 4 times per year with an average of 12 communicants. In 1841 there were about 16 communicants. When the new Church was built it was furnished with a communion table and appropriate vessels for the Eucharist. During Hodgkinson's time there was a succession of assistant curates, whose stipends were paid by a donation from Mrs Anderton of Burley House. It was the first of these, Rev W.G. Wilkinson, who lived in Burley, and, according to Rev Charles Black, was the first clergyman actually to reside here[12].

After Edmund Hodgkinson, the next two Perpetual Curates appointed to St. Mary's, were Rev Frederick Langhorne from 1848 to 1852 and Rev H.G. Robinson 1852 to 1854. We have no information about Langhorne and his pastoral work in Burley, but he was responsible for the return of information required by the 1851 Religious Census, which we will comment on later. Rev H.G. Robinson became the incumbent in 1852 for two years. These were quite dramatic years in the village because the new millowners, William Fison and William Edward Forster, had begun to make improvements in the poor state of health and housing. Robinson took the chair of the Sanitary Committee appointed to deal with health improvements. It was quickly realised that the Committee had no power or funds to make the necessary changes in water supply and drainage. Yet something had to be done because there were outbreaks of cholera and consumption. Through his chairmanship and the drive of the millowners an approach to the Board of Health in London was made, seeking an official inspection of the situation. William Ranger, the Inspector, came to Burley in January 1854, and through his recommendation Burley was allowed to elect a Local Board of Health with powers to collect rates and pay for necessary improvements[13].

This was a period of great change for the Anglican Church in general. As

Frances Knight points out: *During the period from about 1800 to 1870 the Church of England underwent a transformation more rapid, dramatic and enduring than any which it had experienced since the Reformation*[14].This happened for several reasons, amongst them being: population movements caused by industrialisation; agitation from and growth in the number of nonconformists; the entry of younger clergy into the Church from such new institutions as Durham University and from a wider social background; and the reforms of central and local government[15]. In particular clergy began to serve one benefice rather than several as populations grew.

Knight notes also that there was a gradual decline of the pre-eminence of the Anglican Church in the nineteenth century. Leading members of congregations, in consequence of this, began to look back to a medieval past, which for them meant a more orderly and God fearing society. This was expressed architecturally in new Church building in Gothic style. In fact there was a spate of new buildings across the country. Between 1831 and 1851 2029 churches were opened, and others were enlarged. Burley's new Church clearly reflects these changes, with its Gothic style and the increase in accommodation, which was an attempt to attract a larger congregation. The hope was probably to instil a greater sense of religious duty and a more disciplined lifestyle amongst the villagers.

However, the new Local Government which was created by the setting up of the Local Board of Health meant that the new Church was no longer, as the old Fairfax Chapel had been, the centre of both the secular and religious community. St. Mary's was just one among five religious foundations (the others being the Wesleyan Methodists in Burley and Woodhead, the Primitive Methodists in Peel Place and the Independents at Salem Chapel) serving the spiritual needs of the population. We have already noted that St. Mary's congregations did not increase as had been hoped.

Concern about the changes in religious activity and affiliations across the country, noted in Knight's book, led to the Religious Census of 1851[16].The Liberal Government of the day hoped to discover not only the proportion of the population who attended, but also the comparative strengths of the various denominations. On the last Sunday in March, which was Mothering Sunday that year, all clergy and ministers were required to fill in a form stating the numbers who had attended their services that day. Copies of the returns for Burley were made available to us some years ago by the Public Record Office, now the National Archives. Table 1 summarises the returns for Burley and Burley Woodhead, which in 1851 had a total population of 1894.

Table 1. 1851 Religious Census Returns for Burley-in-Wharfedale & Woodhead
The figures in brackets show Sunday School attendances.

	St. Mary's	Wesleyan Methodists	Salem	Primitive Methodists	Wesleyans Woodhead
Total Seats	507	526	450	70	166
Morning	53 (45)	120 (62)	58 (78)	No service (44)	No service
Afternoon	92 (52)	67 (-)	No service	35 (27)	45
Evening	No service	164 (-)	83 (-)	72 (-)	No service

There were enough seats in the five places of worship for virtually the whole population. The overall total attendances were 1097. We do not how many of these were people or children who had attended more than once. Optimistically we can say 60 percent of the population of the village attended a place of worship that day. Various attempts were made to arrive at acceptable figures for attendances. Horace Mann, who was given the official task of compiling the results for the whole country, decided wherever possible to take morning congregation figures as a base, and to add only half the number from the afternoon congregations and a further third from the evening attendances. Then, having deducted 30 percent of the total population for those who could not be expected to attend a church or chapel because of age, ill-health or work commitments, he calculated that 58 percent of those who were able to do so had attended a service that Sunday. Just over half of these had gone to a Church of England service. If we apply this reckoning to Burley, 55 percent of those who were eligible had attended a place of worship, a figure not too far away from the national average.

Anglicans represented only one quarter of the attendances in Burley, which was rather humiliating for the Incumbent and for a Church that regarded itself as the Church of England. Without the Sunday Scholars the figures were even more cause for concern. There has to be some doubt too whether the Census returns were entirely accurate. Two returns were made that day from St. Mary's. A Churchwarden, J.W. Scriven, made one return at the request of Rev Frederick Langhorne, and the Incumbent himself another. The Churchwarden remarked that he was making the return because Mr. Langhorne did not wish to make one to the locally appointed officer. Mr. Langhorne in his return remarked that "he has been desirous to meet the wishes of Her Majesty's Registrar General in every way in his power, though not legally obliged. He forwards this direct on account of the Income being stated in full". There were discrepancies between the two documents. The Churchwarden gave 507 as the official number of seats in Church, whereas the Incumbent cited a smaller figure of 400. The Churchwarden wrote that 75 persons attended morning services and the Incumbent 101.

In the case of all the other places of worship, there was only one return, so that there is at least no ambiguity about them[17]. Generally we have to assume that St. Mary's had not attracted the proportion of villagers for which the sponsors and fund raisers for the new Church had hoped. The Methodists and Independents were obviously providing a welcome alternative to the Established Church, and it was this situation that faced Rev Charles Ingham Black when he began his 41 year ministry at St. Mary's in Burley in 1855.

CHAPTER TWO

REVEREND CHARLES INGHAM BLACK

*Throughout the length and breadth of the country every township should
have a church and a clergyman independent of every other clergyman,
except his Bishop and those lawfully above him.*

Rev. Dr. Black, 1875

After Rev Frederick Langhorne left Burley in 1855, there seems to have
been a short interregnum which was covered by a Curate of Bradford, Rev.
William Faussett Black. He was the older brother of Rev. Charles Ingham
Black, who became perpetual curate and incumbent of St. Mary's in
November 1855. The family came from Sligo, Ireland where Charles was
born in September 1821. Both brothers were graduates of Trinity College
Dublin where they were distinguished scholars, eventually being awarded
Doctorates of Divinity. Charles took his B.A. in 1845 and was ordained
deacon the same year by the Bishop of Tuam in Galway. He was priested
the following year by the Bishop of Kilmore in the West of Ireland. He
came to London in 1849 as curate of St. Anne's, Soho, and served in two
other London parishes, Homerton and Poplar up to 1855, before coming to
Burley[18]. He married Ann Allan, a daughter of a gentleman from Clapton
in July that same year. She was 17 years old.

Black and his young wife arrived in Burley in August 1855 and were able
to move into a new spacious vicarage, which had been built in the previous
two years[19]. They quickly settled into creating a family. Three children,
John, Edith and Anne were born in the next five years and are registered in
the returns of the 1861 Census of Population. Among their servants then
was a young nurse from London. Two others, the cook and the house
maid, were recruited locally. Later Census records suggest and
descendants in New Zealand claim, that they had fifteen children, the
youngest, Ladbroke Lionel, being born in 1878. Not all survived to
adulthood, but six unmarried daughters and two sons were living with
them in the Vicarage in 1891 (when it is noticeable that they had no

living-in servants)[20]. The eldest son, John William Allan Black, married in 1886 Claire Delius, the sister of the composer, Frederick Delius. Herbert Lancelot Ingham Black, born in 1871, migrated to Australia and it is from his descendants that some of the family information has been gathered.

As we indicated earlier Black was a prolific writer and we are fortunate to have many records of his ministry in Burley. These are collected in his *Historical Memorials*, but do not cover all of his forty one years. With the addition of some handwritten notes and press cuttings they cover the period up to 1880. (There are some more recent handwritten notes inserted by Frank Newbould who was the custodian of the book for many years.) There are letters and sermons, some from the very beginning of his ministry, which show his ardent desire to bring parishioners to a deeper spiritual understanding and practice of their faith. The following is taken from his first Advent sermon:

> *Oh my dear Parishioners, as I must give account for you, let me implore you at this sacred season to consider whether you are in the way [of] the Lord Jesus........ Do you by sacred devotion, and spiritual meditation climb up to see the King in His Beauty? Do you daily seek instruction in His Written Word? Do you bring your Children to be Baptized? Do you come to the Lord's Table? Do you observe Family Prayer? Do you make your Servants attend their Christian duties? Do you help the Poor? In these things will the Lord abundantly bless you[21].*

This too was his message a year later in an address 'to Each and All the Inhabitants of Burley and Menston':

> *Persuade yourselves that there is a growing worldliness in all classes; that the inordinate attention paid to intellectual and social pursuits leaves little room for anxiety about Eternal interests; that vice, self will, and vanity, were never more unchecked......I charge you in the sight of God to remember the*

Day of Christ; and to return and live for Jesus[22].

His approach was evidently that of an evangelical Christian. Historians of the Church of England note that there were two major movements in Anglicanism at this time, Evangelicalism and Ritualism. The former came from the Wesleyan revival of the late eighteenth century and the latter took its inspiration from the Oxford Movement of the nineteenth century. As Knight points out 'there was often much more complexity in the religious life of communities' than is suggested by this dichotomy[23]. Other aspects of Black's ministry particularly in the extension and refurbishment of St. Mary's in 1870 suggest that he was also inspired by the more ritualistic ideas of the day.

Rather than trying to recreate chronologically his years in Burley, we will describe some of his main concerns and the far reaching changes which occurred during his incumbency. Parish boundaries were altered, the Church was refitted and extended and finances put on a more secure footing.

THE CHURCH AND ITS FINANCES

On 25th February 1856, only a few months after he had been inducted in early November, Burley was separated from the Parish of Otley. The boundaries of the new Parish covered Burley, Menston, Woodhead and Stead, which had a combined population of about 2500. No doubt Dr. Black and his Church Wardens would be relieved that a considerable portion of the Church income was no longer to be sent to the mother Church in Otley. As it was, he found that the Church was in debt at the moment he arrived. An amount of over £32 was owed on the organ in the Church balcony; debts on the Choir and School amounted to over £51; and £20 was needed to cover repairs in the National School. Fortunately he had the support of the two millowners, Fison and Forster, in clearing these amounts. He himself paid for the Altar to be raised out of his own stipend, which, in a letter written much later, to a former churchwarden, Frederick W. Fox, was only £140 per year[24].

24

Meeting the costs of the Church seems to have dominated his early years. There was a new clock in the Church tower, set going in 1855. Further improvements were considered necessary for the organ, new psalters and hymn books were required in 1856 and gas lighting was installed in 1858. The Church was redecorated in 1860. For all these things, donations were requested, and Dr. Black meticulously records every subscription. Invariably the names of the millowners, Fison and Forster, appear among the biggest donors, but he also includes the widow's mite. He reports extensively in *Historical Memorials* on financial matters.

> *In 1856 the area of the Parish was nearly doubled and the church rate was lost; I, but not in consequence of this, was struck down by fever. As soon as it was necessary, and I could bestir myself again, we opened a subscription list; and in this unsatisfactory manner we raised the money needed for Church purposes in lieu of the rate. But in the second year of this subscription list it failed. I found myself without anyone to collect the subscriptions; and I had already exceeded my own share, and had besides at that time to bear the most depressing burden of all the financial responsibilities of the Burley and Menston schools....It was upon this, that appealing to my Master, and without conferring with flesh and blood, I commenced the divinely instituted and ecclesiastically ordained order of the Weekly Offertory[25].*

At the same time he abolished pew rents (which had traditionally supplemented an incumbent's income) taking instead 'a tithe-charge (a tenth) on the Offertory: and as the tenants changed I gradually raised the glebe-rents, in all £10'. So he also improved his own income as well as that of the Church. He needed to, however, since despite all the subscriptions, for the first few years he was subsidising the running of the Church from his own income. His printed Church financial statements for 1860, 1861 and 1862 show deficits of expenditure over income of £11, £23 and £24, which were large sums in those days. To eke out his stipend and support his growing family, he used his skills as a writer and published several articles and poems which brought him a little income. In 1867 he went to Darmstadt in Germany, to act as Chaplain to the English there. It is not clear how long this was for, but he certainly continued to minister there and gain extra income until he, in his own words, was driven out by the onset of the Franco-Prussian War in 1870. Darmstadt was the seat of the Grand Duke of Hesse Darmstadt, whose son Louis had married Princess Alice, the second daughter of Queen Victoria. Speight in his account of the Parish in his book *Lower Wharfedale* notes that 'he was brought into very kindly and intimate relations with ... Princess Alice'[26]. The Parish was left in the good hands of an assistant Curate and the vicarage was let.

Ever the innovator, no doubt based in prayerful consideration, he organised a committee to look into the extension of the Church and to replace the pews with open benches. His churchwardens, Robert John Hudson and Robert Fox, along with James Grunwell, William Brayshay and Thomas Emsley, other leading parishioners, saw to the employment of architects and lawyers in order to obtain the Faculty to carry out these works[27]. The Faculty and a license were granted on 28th January 1869 and £1000 was deposited with the diocese as a surety that the work would be done properly. The documents were signed, counter signed and witnessed, by all parties including the Bishop of Ripon's registrar, the patron Mrs Sophie Crofton of Burley Hall, as well as the members of the Burley committee and the Vicar. In the case of the last, his signature was witnessed by the British Chargé d'Affaires in Darmstadt.

The works which were permitted to be carried out included:
1. Taking down and entirely removing the east end wall of the small Chancel and its roof.
2. Extending the Chancel to the east by 20 feet.
3. Building an organ chamber in the new Chancel on its north side.
4. Using the south side for a vestry and a water closet.
5. Removing remains of deceased persons buried at the east end of the Church.

6. Resiting the organ from the west end gallery to the new chamber.
7. Removing all existing pews, stalls and sittings, so that they could be replaced by pinewood benches, both in the nave and in the gallery. (Due recognition of the rights of members of the congregation to sit in particular seats had to be allowed, even though no pew rents were collected.)
8. Providing a new pulpit and reading desk.
9. Improving the heating of the Church.

During the rebuilding, any materials from the Church that could not be used again could be sold off towards the expense of the rebuilding. No specific permission was sought or granted for removing the gallery, but in the very detailed instructions to the carpenter, it said 'take down so much of the gallery as may be directed, refix front and make good'. In the event for whatever reason the gallery was entirely removed. It is possible that a fire in the tower during the rebuilding in November 1869 made it unsafe. Certainly the clock and bell were damaged and had to be repaired at a cost of £186.

There was no instruction, either, about removing and replacing windows, except that the new east end was to have the Gothic arched window frame which we see today. The windows in the 1843 east end were three lancet windows, and presumably the stained glass from them was put into the lancets on the south wall, where they are today. They are the three windows next to the Virgin Mary window[28].

The cost of the rebuilding amounted to just over £1971. This amount was achieved through Sunday offerings and other collections. Fifty seven subscribers or groups of subscribers are listed in *Historical Memorials* (p.20-21, with donations in 1869 ranging from 1 shilling and six pence (from A. Friend) to £300 from Robert J. Hudson (Moorville, Woodhead), £375 from William Forster, £400 from Thomas Emsley (Burley Grange) and £429 10s from William Fison. Some of these had already contributed similar sums in a previous appeal in 1868.

Work on the church went on apace. The improvements were commenced on Monday, April 12, 1869 and the "Resanctifying" occurred at the celebration of the Eucharist on Sunday 2nd January 1870 at 8 in the morning. Special services with visiting preachers were held throughout January and these culminated later in the year with the visit of the Bishop of Ripon in August. Numerous gifts were made to mark this refurbishment. The East Window was given as a memorial to Thomas Horsfall of Burley Hall by his family. A south window showing the Virgin was presented by the Emsleys of Burley Grange. A communion kneeling carpet was the gift of Mrs Black and 'the ladies of Darmstadt'. Copies of the Ancient and Modern Hymn Book for the use of the congregation were also given at this time.

All the seating in the Church was free except for three rows on the north side of the nave, which were reserved for the girls of the Sunday School and three on the south for the boys. Parishioners were advised of the times of Services which would be held both during the week and on Sundays. Mattins and Evensong were said daily. On Sundays, Holy Communion was celebrated at 8 o'clock and at 11.15 a.m., Mattins was at 10.30 a.m., and Evensong at 6 p.m.

Thereafter, the finances of the Church seemed to be more secure and attendance at services definitely increased, especially Communion. Attention was turned to the interior of the Church, which was 'painted in fresco' early in 1874. This was paid for by William Fison. On Lady Day (25th March), in the week before Holy Week that year, a whole day of celebration was held in the presence of the Lord Bishop of Ripon to mark the reopening. Communion was celebrated at 5 a.m. and 10.30 a.m. A service of confirmation was held at 2 p.m. and Evensong with a sermon by the Bishop was at 6.45 p.m. The day after the Vicar gave a lecture on the subjects represented in the frescoes.

We can suggest that Dr. Black, in bringing about these changes in St. Mary's was responding like many others in the Anglican Church to influences which Frances Knight has outlined in her study of the nineteenth century church. She notes that with the gradual decline of the pre-eminence of the Anglican church in that century, some began to look back to

the medieval parish church, and the orderly, God fearing society with which they associated it, as a most potent emblem

6. Copy of the poster advertising the reopening in March 1874.

of the world they were losing. The high evaluation of all things medieval – a feature of the Gothic revival – was partly responsible" for a spectacular spate building new churches ... Many thousands were also enlarged or repewed. It was an extraordinary example of middle class philanthropy. If they were nostalgic for the medieval village church, the middle classes were utilitarian about the function of the church in the industrial [areas].... They made an explicit link between church going and the disciplined behaviour that they wished to instil in the lower orders[29].

S. Gunton

In reality the church became a resort for the devout rather than a resource for the community. The emphasis on the Eucharist was a notable feature of this trend. Dr. Black records the number of communicants in his *Historical Memorials.* In the three years from 1855 there had been 715 and in the three years from 1870, 4127.

Like many other churches, St. Mary's continued to be used, if

7. Nave of St. Mary's after the redecoration with frescoes.

30

not regularly by the majority of villagers, for its occasional offices, such as baptism, confirmation, marriage and burial. Providing these rites of passage was not however sufficient in the Vicar's estimation. He was certainly keen to question the continuing expansion of other churches in the village. The first pamphlet contained in *Historical Memorials* is an impassioned plea 'To the Parishioners of Burley' in 1864. It was issued freely and really addressed to the Wesleyans who were proposing to build a new church. Many members of his congregation had been asked to contribute, though not him, and he felt he had leave 'to say a few words'. He points out that as priest in the parish, he had the duty of care for all. Why then was it necessary to build a big new church when the Parish Church could hold most if not all the villagers who wanted to worship? (If not at one sitting, then at two, he had to admit.) He claims that Wesley too declared 'that to forsake the Church would be to incur the loss of God's favour'. If we are not united then we fail the world around us that is not yet Christian. 'Surely it is not the way to give effect to the divine prayer of the great Bishop of our souls, to transmit to those who shall come after us, the humiliating proofs of our miserable squabbles and dissensions'. The Methodist Church was built and opened in 1867, nevertheless. Designed in Gothic style by the architects, Lockwood and Mawson, famous for prestigious buildings in Bradford, it was larger and could accommodate more people than St. Mary's. There is an oral tradition, nowhere substantiated however, that Rev Dr. Black used to walk down Main Street, after the Church was built, with eyes averted from it. The bitterness which this behaviour undoubtedly created is not recorded. Perhaps he did not hear or care to notice it. In the way he defined his own role, he felt obliged to reach out not only to non-believers but also to non-Anglicans in arranging for a Mission to the Village in 1875.

The two missioners engaged for the Mission sent out a pamphlet urging repentance of sins to all villagers. It ended with the prayer that 'God's blessing might rest upon the Mission for His greater glory and the ingathering of many souls'. The Mission lasted from 24th October to 1st November 1875, and we have an account of it written after the event in the Journal of the 18 year old Frances Arnold-Forster of Wharfeside. She writes that before it began the village had been divided into Sections and visitors were to call on every household. Frances and her older sister Florence were given Peel Place to visit. They were quite new to this sort of thing, she says, but they readily did the visiting. Some people welcomed them, but others did not want to know. Some may have found the presence on their doorstep of the two young ladies from Wharfeside a little intimidating!

When the week was over Frances wondered if it had done any lasting good in the village. She felt that it brought people together and differences were set aside. Dissenters joined willingly in the special services held in St. Mary's Church. At the service on 31st October the Church was full to overflowing but during it, to her surprise, one of the missionaries got up and "made a very violent attack upon the Dissenters" - it was the only time that such a thing happened, for they had been warned not to do so — but 'happily a good many of the people seemed hardly to have taken in the full meaning of what he said, so perhaps less harm was done than we feared'. She hints too at other times that differences of opinion were aired, and some long standing grievances about local employment were temporarily set aside. Subsequently one hundred people joined the Bible Class, a Mothers' meeting was started and there was an increase in the number of communicants. However, the Bible Class did not last long. One reason for its failure, Frances commented, was that 'Mr. Black [was] not naturally the right sort of person to conduct such a class'. She also notes that Mr. Black took very little part in the Mission. He was suffering from erysipelas, 'brought on by anxiety about the success of the mission'. In the very last service on 1st Nov, however, he took part and spoke some 'very beautiful words, affirming his willingness to serve the village'[30].

About the time of the Mission Charles Black wrote a summary of the financial situation of the Church in his first twenty years:

The gross settled income of the parish, £87 in 1855, has been increased by £57, partly by raising grants, partly by

endowments of £39 (yearly) in 1861, partly by the sale of land.... The abolition of the church rate (1856), pew rents (1859) and the entire enfranchisement of the Church (1870) has materially promoted its efficiency. The Local difficulties of the Church may in great measure be attributed to the fact that till 1837, no clergyman resided here, that in the years 1835 – 1855, there were five successive chaplains (the clergyman became Incumbent in 1856 and Vicar in 1868) and the Holy Eucharist was not administered here until 1836. Hence towards building the Church (1841 – 3) only £460 – or scarcely one fifth – was raised in the Township; towards building the vicarage only £490 – or scarcely one third – was raised in the Township, of which £420 was given by the Patron. The whole amount raised 1841 – 1875 in all for the Church buildings and the Vicarage, enlarging the Church and in Easter Offerings, is not in excess of £7000*. In the same time towards Minsters' stipends and building of Chapels in the Township, the dissenters have raised little short of £11,000.
* This total is exclusive of £1200 contributed to the National School[31].

We have no further direct evidence that the financial situation of the Church got any less worrying for him during the next twenty years. The Vestry Book records the annual financial statements up to the time of his death in 1896 and these show no great increase in annual income from the offertory or from other donations. In 1871 the annual income was stated to be £311, in 1882, £316 and in 1892, £337. In 1892 expenditure was £12 more than income. Most of the annual accounts, whatever the financial position, show grants to Missions such as SPG and SPCK, the National Society (towards the upkeep of Church Schools) and other worthy causes. Such charitable giving was the duty of the Church. It was obviously painful to him when in 1878 he had to report that 'for the first time in twenty three years, no grant has been made to the Missions of the Church'. He felt it necessary to remind all members of his congregation that they should feel obliged to give more regularly[32].

There were other reasons for the Vicar to be worried. His personal finances still caused him and his large family difficulties. In the letter to F.W. Fox, a former Churchwarden, previously referred to, he complains that 'despite all my efforts and the improvement in income, it is still not enough for me and my family to live on'[33]. There were ten in his family at that time and his private means ('almost exhausted') were devoted solely to educational purposes. He also had accumulated some debts, which fortunately the Churchwardens were able to repay. His parochial responsibilities from 1856 had always extended to Menston and Woodhead, causing him frequent financial problems.

THE PARISH AND ITS BOUNDARIES

The proposal to separate Menston from Burley and the creation of a new parish there seems to have originated in the early 1870s. The foundation stone for St. John's Church was laid in 1870 and the Church was consecrated in 1871. No doubt the Menston parishioners would want it to be their Parish Church. In 1875 he was troubled by protests from Menston that the partition was not taking place fast enough. Some of the Menston ratepayers had petitioned the Bishop of Ripon claiming that Black had devoted too little time and attention to the village. He, they said, had put his private interests before theirs, and made little effort to attract more villagers into the Anglican congregation, so strengthening the power of the dissenters. The Bishop asked for Black's observations on the charges, and, as often was the case, he had his observations printed. He listed all that he had done as priest and provider of education (both Day and Sunday). He had found a man willing to be their priest, but he claimed that such were the conflicts between people in Menston that the man found a living elsewhere. Principally it is claimed by Black that there were unending arguments about who should be the patrons of the new Church, and that those who most wanted the separation had not done enough to provide a sound financial basis for the Parish of Menston. Indeed Black himself had, he claims, sacrificed his own income in the cause of providing services and schooling in Menston. In *Historical Memorials* a press cutting is attached dating from this time advertising the vacancy at Menston:

34

SOLE CHARGE, will be made a VICARAGE, suited to
a Priest with means. Population 600. Healthy, picturesque,
cheap. Church new. Site for Vicarage. Stipend, till
Endowment, small. TITLE might be given.
Address, Vicar of Burley-in-Wharfedale, Leeds.

Undoubtedly composed by Black himself, the advertisement suggests that
private means were essential at that time for the running of Menston
Church, but that it was a cheap area in which to live. Eventually all the
legal and ecclesiastical requirements were met and the Parish of Menston
and Woodhead was carved out of the combined Parish. Dr. Black gives the
date of its creation as 28th April 1876. Even with Menston and Woodhead
taken out of the Burley Parish, there was still a large stretch of upland for
the Vicar to oversee. The boundary ran (and still runs) up Moor Lane to
the triangle, and all the people living west of that line as far as the

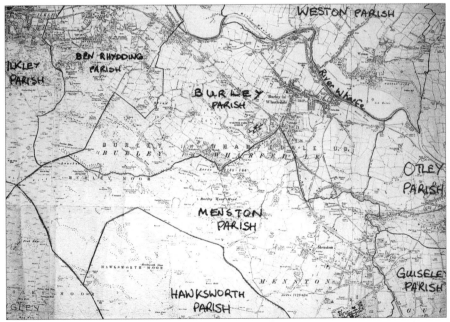

8. Sketch map showing
the parish boundaries on the base of an Ordnance Survey map of 1910.

35

boundary of Ben Rhydding and Ilkley were in Burley Parish. Apart from small farms the only settlement of any kind was the hamlet of Stead. In 1873, we gather from a remaining handbill which had been circulated to the inhabitants in that area, services were regularly held at Mount Stead House on Sundays and Fridays. This venture was to be extended through the acquisition of a small wooden chapel, to seat about 60. It would be dedicated to St Mary Magdalene. However, the whole venture does not seem to have come to fruition, but it is another indication that Dr. Black was willing to make every effort to offer the Anglican faith to the people living in his parish[34]. There was also a financial reason for keeping in touch with as many parishioners as possible, for while some of his monetary worries were taken away from him when Menston and Woodhead were separated from Burley, the loss of 600 potential givers from his Parish could not be ignored.

The increase in population in Burley during Black's time led obviously to a growing number of funerals, and burial space around the Church was proving inadequate. On December 4th 1884, an extraordinary meeting of village ratepayers was held. The purpose was to agree to the purchase of a site for a new burial ground. The proposal was that the field known as Cockridding in Bradford Road should be the site. There had been some concern about the distance from the main village, but according to the Vicar it was the only suitable ground that could be procured. 'The complaint that the ground is *very* distant is made in forgetfulness *how rarely* (it is to be hoped) any of us will be called to travel it'. God's Acre was consecrated on Thursday 5th February 1885. The total cost was £1270 19s and Walter Bairstow, the Church Warden had been treasurer. A bier, available for rich and poor without fee, had been donated by Miss Fanny Hargreaves of Langford House.

Throughout Black's incumbency Churchwardens played a large role in the administration of Church affairs. Some of them have already been named in the text. (All of them are listed in Appendix Three.) Most of them served for a short time, the average being about two years. There were two wardens, one chosen by the incumbent and the other by the lay members of the congregation. From 1867 they were known as the Vicar's Warden and the People's Warden. One man, Robert Fox, served as People's Warden from 1869 until after Black's death. There is a plaque in memory of him on the west wall of the Church. We know from Census records that he was born in Burley in 1834 and was the brother of Frederick William Fox. He had been the People's Warden for two years prior to Robert, and he was the one to whom Charles Black wrote about his financial difficulties. Robert was listed as a grocer and commercial traveller in 1871, living in a cottage not far from the Church. Later we know that he lived in Elm Grove.

Among the wardens there were young men and older men, men of property, professionals, industrialists and tradesmen. Representatives from the larger houses such as Robert Hudson of Moorville at Woodhead, John Rouse of Burley House, and Reginald Summers Yorke of Burley Hall, feature as Vicar's wardens. Edward Penrose Arnold (who later changed his name to Arnold-Forster) was in his early twenties when he became Vicar's warden in 1874. The adopted son of W.E. Forster and his wife Jane, he had recently become a Director of Greenholme Mills. Thomas Clark was Vicar's warden in 1860 when also in his early twenties. He was the Headmaster of Greenholme Mills School from 1856 until it was closed in 1897. Harold Hebblethwaite was twenty eight when he became Vicar's warden in 1891. He was a village doctor living at Dial House and also Medical Officer of Health for the Burley Local Board. On his appointment as Vicar's warden in 1878, John Lupton was thirty seven. He was a village butcher, with a shop in Main Street near to the Queen's Head. In *Historical Memorials* he is mentioned as organising parish events and fund raising activities. (We will refer to him later in the time of Dr. Black's successor.) James Stradling had worked his way up from being the son of a mill worker, who had migrated with his family from Wellington in Somerset in the 1850s. He became Vicar's warden in 1893 when he had reached the age of fifty three. By this time James had become an official of the Local Board, responsible for rent and tax collection. Of course there were no women; they would not be considered eligible at this time.

THE CHURCH SCHOOL[35]

9. Thomas Clark

When Rev. Charles Ingham Black came to St. Mary's Church in 1855, he found the National School that had been opened in 1837 in dire straits:

So embarrassed are the funds, that there was not enough in hand in August (1855) to pay the half-year's salary, due June 25th, to the Master and Mistress.

He decided to devote himself to managing the school more effectively and many of his carefully printed annual reports are in the Church records. He had to concern himself with fund-raising and more efficient management. He opened a subscription list, and had plans to build a house for a school master as an enticement to a 'good' head, who might also look for extra income from evening classes, as well as bring in more day pupils. At the same time, not unlike some of his twentieth century successors, he approached 'big business'. William Fison and Company agreed to pay off the outstanding debt. By these means he hoped to achieve

...a good Village school, where the children of a large and respectable class not engaged in mill labours, or not intending that their children should be so engaged, may receive an education of the better order....The Schools cannot be called very prosperous at present. A great improvement, however, in this respect, may be looked for, consequent upon the establishment of Messrs. Fison and Co.'s projected schools at Greenholme, which, besides promoting the cause of education in the township, will enable the National School to assert its proper character as the School of the Village.

What Black meant by this phrase *The School of the Village* is not entirely

38

clear. At least a third of the households in Burley were involved in mill work at that time and sent their children to Greenholme Mills School. Most of the other households, too, could be described as belonging to the working class. So, what did he mean by the 'large and respectable class'? He certainly did not send his own children to the school. Presumably he fell in with the norms of Victorian society which dictated that his class would send its children to private schools or would have them tutored at home. There was also his continued concern that all Christians should be united in the Anglican fold and attendance at the National School would be a move in that direction. Whoever he thought the National school was intended for, we do know that its subsequent history shows a somewhat chequered progress for reasons often outside his control. Buildings had to be maintained and improved and teachers recruited who had the ability to educate the pupils to the required government standards. Moreover pupils had to be encouraged to attend regularly, and parents satisfied that their weekly fees were not being wasted. Year by year subscribers and other donors had to be persuaded that their money was being used to good effect. It would have been difficult to achieve satisfactory outcomes in all of these.

By the mid-1870s the Inspectors were repeatedly warning the managers that if the Infants were not taught in more suitable surroundings, the Government grant to the school would be reduced. Three reports in a row were very critical of the Infants' classroom. Black had no option but to get the managers to act. He had plans drawn up and approached the trustees for the extra funding. Subscriptions towards the new buildings in the year 1877-78 raised a sum to meet the cost of these at just over £154. After the extensions and additions were completed, the principal classroom had been enlarged and a partition erected to allow for infants to be taught in a larger area. Improvements were made to the playground space and the 'offices', which then had a patent flushing system. At the next inspection some appreciation of the changes was expressed.

.....The infants whom I examined did better than at the last inspection, and still more improvement will be shown next

*year. A new room, I am very glad to notice, for the use of the
infants has been added to the school. General improvement
will be expected in elementary subjects and also in the
needlework next year.*

Throughout the rest of Black's incumbency, there were further repairs and
minor alterationsto the Back Lane School, usually requiring appeals to
donors and subscribers, but the building essentially remained the same. By
1895 Black was able to show that he had balanced the books and, in what
was to be his valedictory report on the School, for he died before another
report was due, he was almost euphoric. His first reason for joy was that an
appeal for funds had been very successful during the year. It was possible,
secondly, that the school would be enlarged 'to meet future possible
governmental requirements', by building a second storey. There was talk
of more financial support for voluntary schools and it was the time of an
upsurge in demand for education beyond elementary. Thirdly, fees payable
by parents had been abolished, and state grants more than made up for the
uncertainties of that source of income. Fourthly, the HMI had bestowed an
accolade upon the school in the annual examination, saying that 'the
school having improved in a striking manner during the last two years'
should receive 'the highest grant which it is in the power of the Inspector
to award'. Black overlooked the fact that there were also criticisms, and
that some of the work 'lacked intelligence'. It was very much a curate's
egg of a report and the award of a higher grant was possibly an
encouragement rather than the last word on the school's achievements.

    However, Charles Ingham Black presumably died happily. The
school had been at the centre of his efforts as Vicar and there was enough
evidence to make him feel contented after a great deal of effort, many
trials and considerable worry. He wrote:

> *Forty years of disparagement, in the most important*
> *department of his whole charge, have contributed greatly to*
> *the sorrows and disappointments which cast the oppressive*
> *shadows of the Cross of God over the whole life ministerial.*
> *Through the long night I have been spared to see the Aurora*

coming up, tho' coming slowly, and the morning breaking forth with its joy. I thank my parishioners, especially my poorer neighbours, who in feeling and in fact have been so munificent, and in union with them, the very many who, however at variance with my ministry, have never once, in all those years, originated in themselves, or their children, any difficulty in the conducting of the School, and have helped me to the last. Most of all I thank the Head Master, and Miss Paley and Miss Tyreman; and in their due order and degree, my dear young friends, Pupil Teacher Bertha Pape, and Hannah Leach, monitress, for their loyal service and their devotion to their duties.

He concluded the report with an intercession for teachers and scholars:

Almighty and Everlasting God and Father, who, by Thy Holy Spirit, dost teach us what alone is worthy of knowledge, grant to all who devote themselves to the instruction of Thy children, that by the same Spirit they may impart to Thy dear little ones, the true wisdom from above, and by their holy obedience to Thy Church and Word, may leave them a bright example to Thy honour and glory, through Jesus Christ our Lord. Amen.

There was no mention of his original aim to create 'the School of the Village', but by now he had perforce come to accept that other schools played their part in the education of the village children. This prayer and his concluding remarks on the National School do seem to imply that his attitudes to the parishioners had mellowed. Over the years he had come to accept that he could not force people into his own Anglican mould and needed to work alongside others in the village[36].

THE END OF DR. BLACK'S MINISTRY

It is not possible to conclude this section on Reverend Charles Ingham

41

Black and the Church without some reference to his prolific writings, poetry, pamphlets, lectures and hymns, throughout his ministry in Wharfedale. In a book of poems *Memorialia Cordis*, which he published in 1856 and dedicated to W.E.F. (William Forster of Wharfeside), he seeks to emulate William Wordsworth with his Lakeland and Wharfedale verses. An example shows that he knew much about our local beauty spots and the history of the valley before he took up his living here.

NIGHT; BARDEN COTTAGE

Sweetest and last of all day's heavenly moods,
These twilight moments. Over moors and fells
Our pathway lay, where many a record tells
Of the good old monastic brotherhoods.
Now all is rest. The stream down glades and dells,
Ever for ever pours its peaceful floods,
Filling, with its sleep-counselling oracles,
The unprofaned recesses of the woods.
Hush ! Voices, vague as echoes, and the bright
Clear stars do tell us with their mellow gleams,
What ages have passed o'er the Barden towers
And ruinous Bolton. The long-faded hours
Will crowd upon our Spirits thro' the night,
And Storied Wharfe will teach us in our dreams[37].

Historical Memorials contains printed leaflets which advertise the talks and sermons which he gave in Burley. For instance in 1872 and 1873 he gave a course of free Lectures in History and Readings in Poetry during the winter months at the National School. Titles included 'The Close of Ancient History', 'The Holy Roman Empire', and 'Poets of the Western World'. It is tantalizing to speculate how many turned up regularly.

Black had received the degree of Doctor of Divinity from Trinity College Dublin. Its library has two of his publications, a volume of poetry of 1843 and another with the title:

'The pneumatomachy of the day: the clergy and the scriptures. A vindication of Holy Writ from the assaults on its integrity and mystery directed by priests and doctors who, within the church, are graduating in the school of a new divinity.' London, 1889[38].

Perhaps a sketch of it is contained in one of the leaflets contained in *Historical Memorials* entitled *The Real Presence of God The Holy Ghost*. This had been his sermon to a gathering of priests, and like most of his published work, begins with a quotation, this time from George Herbert, priest and poet,

> *And art thou grieved, sweet and sacred Dove;*
> *Grieved for me? The God of Strength and Power,*
> *Almighty God doth grieve; He puts on Sense!*
> *I'm not to my grief alone,*
> *But to my God's too: He doth groan!*

'We are in great danger' he writes 'of overlooking …. the gifts, or supernatural endowments, and the graces of habitual moral qualities bestowed or engrafted on the Christian by the HOLY SPIRIT.' He then argues in great detail how we cannot be Christians without acknowledging the gift of the Holy Spirit to the Apostles at Pentecost. In resounding phrases he claims that all Christians are falling into the same heresy. In the Church of England 'the Apostolic light has paled before the intense flame of the gospel of Commerce'. Catholics, Protestant dissenters, and those who support the Arianism of Ireland and the Unitarianism of England, all deny 'the Real Presence of the Holy Ghost'. His plea is to confirm our faith in the Holy Trinity which is based in a true reading of the Scriptures[39].

Dr. Black was clearly a priest with very strongly held views about theological subjects on which he was willing to expound not only in the pulpit but also in print to a wider public. His views may seem very old fashioned to us who have been honed a century later by changes in society and religion. It would be difficult for a priest in Burley today to send a letter to 'the women of the West Riding of all estates and conditions' proclaiming it to be DEADLY SIN (sic) when persons unmarried act to one

43

another as if married and do not make a secret of it. 'Yet it is to be seen in the cottage: the innocent daughter of the parsonage sees it when she calls'. He concludes 'I beseech you to hear this word of exhortation.....and endeavour to lessen the evil in this land.'[40].

In accordance with the practice of separating men and women (they used to sit on opposite sides of the nave, women on the north side and men on the south) he also gave a lecture to the men on the sin of "soliciting". He promoted the establishment of a branch of the Church of England Temperance Society, at a meeting chaired by Edward P. Arnold (later Arnold-Forster) in July 1876. Sin was invariably the theme of his sermons and lectures in Advent and Lent, and perhaps above all he felt the greatest was the sin of disunity among Christians. In 1876 he wrote 'it is the great Passion-Prayer of the Lord Jesus, that we all may be one'. He despaired about the divisions in the Church, but perhaps as he grew older he came to realise that ecumenical changes would only come slowly.

It may sound from what has been written earlier that there were no times when enjoyment entered into the Church calendar. That would be wrong, for clearly he encouraged the parish to get together for social gatherings. Fund raising bazaars took place regularly and there were socials at Christmas and Shrovetide which are noted in *Historical Memorials*. The National School was used for Entertainments such as that which took place on Saturday, 28th December in 1872. Tea and entertainment by the Choir and various members of the congregation cost one shilling, and it was possible just to go for the entertainment in the evening at six pence.

The strength of his faith shines through in all of his hymns. The words of five suitable for use at the Eucharist were published in a Hymn Book called *Lyra Eucharistica* edited by Rev. Orby Shipley, in 1864. Of these the one entitled *Creative Word* would still seem most relevant today. Its last verses are:

> O Jesu God, Jesu Man,
> Thou, Lord of Power and might,
> Didst love us ere our life began,

Dost love us day and night:

Come! Jesu, through Thy Spirit come!
That we may come through Thee,
And dwell in our Dear Father's Home
through all Eternity[41].
The metre is such that it fits perfectly to the hymn tune *Gerontius* by J. B.
Dykes or *Richmond* by T. Haweis. We wonder which Dr. Black would
have preferred.

One of his Christmas Carols is commemorated in the stained glass window
on the south side of the Church, which was commissioned soon after his
death:

'Twas in the winter cold, when earth
Was desolate and wild,
That angels welcomed at His birth
The everlasting Child.
From realms of ever bright'ning day,
And from His throne above
He came with humankind to stay,
All lowliness and love.

Then in the manger the poor beast
Was present with his Lord;
Then swains and pilgrims from the East
Saw, wondered, and adored.
And I this morn would come with them
This blessèd sight to see,
And to the Babe of Bethlehem
Bend low the reverent knee.

But I have not, it makes me sigh,
One offering in my power;
'Tis winter all with me, and I
Have neither fruit nor flower.
O God, O Brother, let me me give
My worthless self to Thee;

And that the years which I may live
May pure and spotless be.

Grant me Thyself, O Saviour kind,
The Spirit undefiled,
That I may be in heart and mind
As gentle as a child;
That I may tread life's arduous ways
As Thou Thyself hast trod,
And in the might of prayer and praise
Keep ever close to God.

Light of the everlasting morn,
Deep through my spirit shine;
There let Thy presence newly born
Make all my being Thine:
There try me as the silver, try,
And cleanse my soul with care,
Till Thou art able to descry
Thy faultless image there[42].

This was published in 1871 in an influential book of Christmas Carols, and
it has been revived in the *Nine Lessons and Carols* services held in Burley
in recent years. Music for it was composed by Joseph Barnby (1838-1896)
a one time chorister of York Minster, who distinguished himself in the
musical world. It is probable that Barnby met Black long before he came
to Burley as they both worked in London in the early 1850s.

His life came to an end after a period of declining health on 29th June 1896
at the age of 74 years. He was the Incumbent of St. Mary's for 41 years,
and made a great mark on the Church and the Parish, through the changes
he initiated. He was laid to rest by the west door at St. Mary's on Thursday
2nd July. Mrs Black and the members of the family still living with her
moved to Torquay.

10. Black Memorial Window with words from his carol.

CHAPTER THREE
DR. BLACK'S IMMEDIATE SUCCESSORS

REV. REGINALD PLUMER STEDMAN, 1896-1903
REV. ERIC REDE BUCKLEY, 1903-1922

A fresh system of Education for the village to be started in the future – either under the auspices of a School Board or of Mr Stedman – the latter being determined to raise sufficient voluntary contributions to carry on a Church School if possible. Florence Arnold-Forster.

I propose during the coming year to set on foot a Parochial Church Council, as I feel strongly that the time has come when the laity as a whole should exercise a larger and more direct influence on the management of Church matters than has been the case in the past. Rev. Eric R. Buckley

Rev. R. Plumer Stedman, born in Cheshire in 1852, graduated from St. John's College Cambridge and was ordained Deacon in 1881 and Priest the following year. He had been a curate at All Saints Blackburn for one year and then moved to Halifax where he spent eight years. Before coming to Burley he had been Vicar of Brighouse from 1890 to 1896. His wife Annie came from Halifax. The census of 1901 shows him at the age of 47 living in the Vicarage with Annie, a niece and three servants. We know very little about him and there seem to be few records to provide details of his churchmanship, his approach to parishioners or his seven years in the village. He inherited a curate from Dr. Black's last year, Rev. Samuel Ross, a young man who had come to Burley in 1895 and must have had quite a difficult time with the illness of Dr. Black and the responsibilities thrown upon him.

One of the first issues that faced Mr. Stedman was an educational dispute in the village caused when Greenholme Mills School, 'the Mill School', was closed in 1897. This school had provided day and evening classes and was initially set up in 1856 to provide education for young millworkers who spent half a day in the mill and half at school. School rooms were at

48

first in mill premises, but in 1868 moved to the Lecture Hall in Main Street, occupying the Annex there. Its Headteacher was Thomas Clark, brought up in the Church of England in Leeds, and Vicar's warden in 1860. The school provided non-denominational religious instruction, because it was affiliated to the British and Foreign Schools Society[43]. The National School, managed by the Vicar and trustees appointed by him, taught a religious curriculum along Church of England lines. The closure of the Mill School meant that there could possibly be no non-denominational education in Burley beyond the Infant stage. There was an Infant School, known as the Township School, which had no religious affiliation. The prospect of a Church of England school for all of Junior age and beyond was the main cause of the dispute which met Mr. Stedman. He probably had no idea how keenly some people felt about this.

The National School in Back Lane had places for less than 200 children, and the Mill School for just over 150. The Township Infant School had places for less than 100. By 1897 the estimate of children needing elementary education was 500 and it was clear that extra school places would have to be found. The Mill Company had financed the Greenholme School with the aid of grants from the Department of Education in London. It had been very much 'the creation and special child of [William and Jane Forster at] Wharfeside for more than 40 years' wrote Florence, the older adopted daughter of the Forsters, in her diary in July 1897 [44].

The reasons why the Mill School was closed in 1897 are not clear, but very probably they were a result of a decline in the use of child labour in the Mills and the increasing relative costs of providing such a school. Thomas Clark, the Headmaster, was also approaching retirement and there were questions of providing him with a pension. The control of Greenholme Mills too was passing to a new generation. William Fison was nearing retirement and his son Fred Fison was very much in charge, along with Edward Arnold-Forster, the adopted son of the late W.E. Forster, the other founder of the company. There was also much discussion in the country at large about the necessity to provide full time education beyond the elementary stages. Up to this point, most new elementary schools were provided by School Boards set up under the Education Act of 1870, which had been formulated and guided through Parliament by the same W.E. Forster. Wherever a need for a school was proved, the legislation allowed for the setting up of School Boards in villages and towns with the power to raise rates to fund schools. Burley had never needed a School Board because of the existence of the National School, the Township School, and the Mill School. With the closure of the last, and the increasing population of the village, there was now a case for setting up a School Board.

This solution was favoured by Fred Fison, who is reported to have asked why the mill should go on paying for a school when there was legislation to provide for it out of public finance. A Board was also supported by local Councillors, especially the forthright Joseph Foulds, a Congregationalist, and members of the non-Anglican churches in the village. What had been the Local Board of Health in Burley had in 1895 been statutorily changed into an Urban District Council with more powers, but not the authority to set up a School Board. That still required Government permission. A School Board School would teach the children a non-denominational curriculum as was the case in Menston. After all it was, they said, the much respected late Mr. Forster of Burley who had guided the legislation through parliament and whose Mill School had taught on non-sectarian lines. On the other hand Mr. Forster's widow, Jane, and her adopted son, Edward, were not convinced that a School Board needed to be introduced, requiring permission from the Department of Education in London, an election campaign and no doubt much acrimony during it. Further there were by 1897, following a parliamentary enquiry, moves towards a new Education Bill which would eventually abolish School Boards and allow scope for large Local Authorities to provide education for the increasing population beyond the elementary stages.

When Mr. Stedman learned of the situation, he thought that a second National School should be built to supplement the provision in the existing one. His fellow managers of the school in Back Lane had long been concerned like Dr. Black about the inadequacies of their buildings and decided that a completely new school, big enough to provide for all the village children, on a different site in the village, was required. Mr. Stedman was converted to their view and became a staunch advocate of that solution to the question of providing for the growing population. During 1897 however those supporting the School Board idea mounted a campaign and in August, after the village had joined in celebrations of the Diamond Jubilee of Queen Victoria, a public meeting was held to debate the issue. The Vicar and National School trustees countered with strong arguments outlining the case for a National School to serve the whole village. A leaflet was distributed around the village before the meeting:

THE EDUCATION QUESTION
IN BURLEY-IN-WHARFEDALE.

Owing to the closing of the Greenholme Mill School, a New School must be built.

School Accommodation for 500 children will be required.

The average cost of building a Board School is £10 per head.

The average cost to Ratepayers for Borrowed Capital, in Interest, Repayment of Loan, and School Maintenance is not less than 19s. 9 3/4d. per child.

If a Board School be erected—

The School Board Rate will amount to about 1 shilling in the £.

Every Ratepayer, even the smallest, in the Township will have to pay his Rate as long as he lives in it.

A man who has educated his own children, will now begin to pay for the education of the children of others.

These drawbacks will be avoided by the erection of a National School.

The larger Ratepayers will for the most part bear the

burden of the cost of the erection of a   National School.
The cost of the Triennial Election, as well as the ill-feeling it often engenders, will be avoided.

The Ministers of the Nonconformist bodies in Burley will have the opportunity of giving the children of Non-conformist parents such religious instruction as they desire, in a class-room to be provided for that purpose.

The Church Catechism will not be taught to the children of Nonconformist parents if not desired.

At the meeting the Vicar spoke at length on the lines of the argument in the leaflet and added the attractive fact that already promises had been made by wealthy residents of £4000 towards the cost of building a National School. An offer of two places on the Committee of Management to Non-conformists in recognition of their needs was also made. The meeting was then addressed by supporters of the School Board but in the end it was decided to call for no action until a further public meeting in September. The records show that the later meeting was better attended and probably followed a strong campaign by the School Board supporters. A resolution at that meeting to request the formation of a School Board in Burley was carried by a large majority and that was forwarded to the Department of Education in London.

The Vicar and the managers of the National School then acted quickly, sending a letter to London with their version of the situation in Burley. They suggested that the September Ratepayers' meeting had not been representative and accused one of the speakers of being a 'paid agitator'. Their own evidence drawn from a house to house survey was that 330 out of 520 had indicated their support for another National School. Also they had gone as far as drawing up plans for a school, acquired a site and raised most of the money to build it. A short time later they sent a letter to the Department of Education requesting permission to proceed with the building, so that it could be ready for October 1898. In the meantime they also took over the empty classrooms in the Lecture Hall, vacated by the

Mill School, and appointed a head master to cover the transition to the new school. Their requests were granted and the Department sent a reply to the counter proposal from the September public meeting, declaring that after careful consideration, a School Board could not be formed.

Expressions of anger at this decision of the Department were made in the Burley Council and at a public meeting in January, Councillor Foulds is reported to have said:

> The decision of the Department was not only an insult to the majority of ratepayers but also a great insult to the memory of the late Mr. Forster.

Some speakers demanded moderation and compromise, and others, also recalling the work of W.E. Forster, spoke of the people's right to be involved in the provision and control of schooling. In the end the meeting carried a resolution protesting against the 'unfair action of the Department' and setting up a committee to take any action that was deemed necessary. Questions were raised in the House of Commons about the situation in Burley, but the Department declined to alter its judgement.

Action to provide an alternative school to the proposed new Anglican one continued during 1898. The non-conformists in the village gained permission to use the Sunday School alongside St. John's Methodist Church in Main Street as a day school for all ages and the Township School for infants. Grants were obtained from the Wesleyan Committee of Education and funds were raised in the village to allow the school to function. The school came to be known as the Wesleyan but religious education was taught on non-denominational lines. Its doors were opened for pupils on 3rd October 1898. The local press dubbed this a victory for the Non-conformists since the new Anglican school was not ready for occupation that day, and though alternative provision was made for the children, it was not until 24th October 1898 that the National School was officially opened with its young headmaster, Richard Gossop.

The National School was built on land given by Edward Arnold-Forster to the Trustees with the proviso that the school was to be used for

the education of children and adults or children only of the
labouring manufacturing and other poorer classes of the said
chapelry of Burley-in-Wharfedale.....in accord with the
principles of the National Society.
At its official opening the platform party consisted of the Vicar and Mrs
Stedman, the curate, Rev. S. Ross, the Lord and Lady of the Manor, Sir
Malby and Lady Crofton, Mrs Jane Forster, widow of W.E. Forster, and
her daughter-in-law and other members of the village elite. They could see
no reason why this architect designed school on its spacious site could not
provide elementary schooling for the whole of the village. Nevertheless the
Wesleyan School continued and eventually became Burley Council School
when the West Riding County Council took it over completely in the early
20th Century. It only closed its doors after the Second World War in 1950.
The National School was an all-age school until 1950, when at last,
renamed as Burley Church of England Primary School, it provided schooling for all village pupils up to the age of eleven[45].

This story indicates very clearly that there was considerable division in
Burley over religious affiliation and practice at the end of the nineteenth
century. How far this was a residue of earlier differences highlighted
during Dr. Black's ministry or a consequence of Mr. Stedman's own
theological and social dispositions is difficult to tell. There was no doubt
of his determination to keep a National School presence in the village, and
of course that had consequences throughout the next century, which we
will review later.

We know little else about Mr. Stedman or his life in Burley. There was no
Parochial Church Council and therefore no minutes. The annual accounts
entered in the Vestry Book, show no great changes from Dr. Black's time.
Robert Fox continued as churchwarden throughout his incumbency, and
John Lupton continued as his parish clerk. We have a little insight from the
Lupton diary of the work he had to do as clerk and therefore some of the
parish activities at that time. John Lupton, a butcher in the village, was
born in 1840 and attended St. Mary's from an early age. He is remembered
in Dr. Black's book (*Historical Memorials)* because he was churchwarden

54

from 1878 to 1884 and was one of the organisers of 'Entertainments' in the National School. Cutting up the ham for the teas was always expected of him, no mean job when we learn that as many as 160 or more sat down for tea on such occasions. He was often the person who took money at the door or at the gates of the gardens of the big houses, where Summer Fetes were held. As Parish Clerk, his duties were to prepare registers for baptisms, marriages and funerals. He had to arrange the purchase of grave plots in the Church yard or at God's Acre, liaising with the Verger and Sexton, George Vine. He banked the Church collections every Monday morning and collected rents due to the Church.

Once he had to go the Court House at Otley on behalf of the Rev. Stedman, who had been summoned for not taking out a licence at the proper time for his dog! John paid the fine of five shillings plus costs of seven shillings and sixpence. Another responsibility was being a Manager of the new National School after it opened in 1898. He went to Church twice or three times each Sunday and, except during holidays, his wife went with him only to Evensong (she would be at home in the mornings cooking the Sunday joint, which would no doubt be of the best cut). He became a member of the Communicants' Guild, set up by the Vicar in 1900, though he records that only three men turned up along with twenty five women at the inaugural meeting[46].

Other church organisations continued throughout this period such as the Sunday School attended by large numbers of village children. A Mother's Union was set up in 1898, as the banner in Church shows, though there had been meetings of Mothers before this, started after the Mission in 1875. Jane Forster noted in a letter she wrote to Florence in Ireland on 1st January 1890 that after a visit to friends, she and Frances called at Cathedine (home of Edward and Edith Arnold-Forster) "to see Edith's tea party for the Mothers". There must have been regular Parish Magazines, though none survive. As we will see later, the magazines for 1903 began with volume number seven, suggesting that Mr. Stedman started the monthly publication of church magazines in 1897.

The Parish Room was also acquired for use by the National School and the Church in 1900. We do not know how far the Vicar was the moving force in this acquisition. The rooms had an uncertain past, possibly an old grammar school dating from the 17th century, but certainly part of old farm buildings at the time of purchase. The rooms had been used by the Local Board of Health for meetings according to Joseph Foulds[47]. After the new National School had been opened, the managers decided to purchase the old farm buildings and the land around them 'to protect the school premises from the possibility of the erection of any undesirable building adjoining the school yard…..it is intended to convert part of the old farm house into a Parish Room, where meetings connected with the Young Men's Friendly Society, the Mothers' Union and any other parochial organisations can be held'. The National School would also be able to use it for cookery lessons[48]. Harry Chorley, an architect living in Woodhead, was probably involved in the purchase and reconstruction of the building which was carried out afterwards. The local press carried an announcement in January 1901 that 'work in the Parish Room is now completed for its intended uses, for parochial affairs and as a school of cookery'[49].

The Boer War in South Africa occurred during Stedman's incumbency, but of its effect on the village and the church we have little information. There is no memorial in St. Mary's, though a plaque was made to honour those who had enlisted for the army, and this is displayed in the Queen's Hall. Just over a decade later a much longer and more violent war was to have a huge impact during the incumbency of Stedman's successor. Interestingly, Eric Rede Buckley, who followed Stedman, had been Vicar of Kirtlington, near Oxford from 1895 to 1902, and this was the parish to which Stedman moved and where he remained until he retired in 1911, when he moved to Bath. We do not know whether there was any reason for the 'swop', and enquiries of the local historian and churchwarden, Margaret Forey, in Kirtlington have not produced any explanation. She has kindly sent us a photograph of Rev. Eric Buckley from her archives.

Rev. Eric Rede Buckley came to Burley in 1902 having been Vicar of Kirtlington in Oxfordshire for seven years previously. He was born in

Paddington, London, in 1866, and graduated from St. John's College Oxford, with a good degree in History in 1889 and in Theology two years later. He was ordained deacon in 1891, and priested the following year. His first parish as curate was in Bodmin moving from there to Kirtlington in 1895. While a curate in Bodmin, Eric married Gertrude, daughter of Dr. James Haworth of Filey, on 17th January 1893 at Saint Oswald's Parish Church Filey. Perhaps his wife persuaded him to come to Yorkshire when an opportunity arose, but we know of no other connections which might have lured them from the south. It is possible that the Arnold-Forsters knew of them. An entry in Florence Arnold-Forster's diaries for November 1903 suggests at least that Wharfeside was pleased with their coming. She writes:

> *I went on to Wharfeside and spent 10 days with Francie, who was still in very frail health....Edith Black was staying with her again at this time but her happiest intercourse was with Mr and Mrs Buckley whose appearance in Burley is nothing less than a Godsend to our Francie, and all who love her.*

A later entry for July 1907 in Florence's diaries also suggests a close connection with them.

> *Francie was going through three or four days of extra strenuous work – over her Examination for the Lambeth Theological Degree.....She and [a friend] have been steadily working for a year with Mr. Buckley as their 'coach' for this severe examination...Francie had not been at all well during this time but...She had been very kindly and considerately helped to get through [the examinations] without breaking down, by her wise friends, Mr. and Mrs. Buckley.....*[50].

We have a very good guide to some of the new Vicar's approach to his work as all the Parish Magazines for 1903 have survived[51]. The magazine was published monthly in 1903, with a blue cover. Inside there were 12 pages of local adverts and parish news surrounding a 32 page inset nationally published called the *Church Monthly*. The margins of the cover consisted of adverts for local firms and shops, surrounding an idealised drawing of the Church. Apart from the Vicar, it gave the names of the Church Wardens, George Wood and Robert Fox, the Organist, F.J. P. Drake, the Clerk, John Lupton and the Verger George Vine. It was priced 1 penny, and the 1903 issues were labelled Volume 7.

In January 1903, the Parish News in the magazine contained a Vicar's Letter, the only one throughout the rest of the year. He noted that he was now without a curate, Mr. Ross, who had moved to Keighley. As a result he wrote:

> I have felt obliged, somewhat reluctantly to abandon many of the week-day services, in order to have as much time as possible for visiting and study, for I am convinced that the man who attempts to preach two sermons a week without ample time for study and preparation is attempting an impossibility.

His further intentions for the Parish were then outlined:

> I propose during the coming year to set on foot a Parochial Church Council, as I feel strongly that the time has come when the laity as a whole should exercise a larger and more direct influence on the management of Church matters than has been the case in the past. I hope at an early date to call together a meeting of all who feel interested in the forming of such a Council.....

An immediate financial objective was to clear off a debt incurred in land purchase when the National School was built and the Parish Room acquired. He also indicated that he wished to form a branch of the British and Foreign Bible Society. Among the Parish Notes in that January issue we read references to the activities of the Girls' Friendly Society, the Sewing Party, the Mothers' Meeting (Mother's Union) and the Sunday School. The last had 306 pupils on its books with average attendances of 85 in the mornings and 131 in the afternoons. The National School held a prize giving with prizes for regular attendance and medals for those who had never missed a day. The funds for this prize giving were contributed by:

> Mrs Edith Arnold-Forster, Miss Frances Arnold-Forster, Mrs Whitaker, Mrs. J. Whittaker, Mrs Butterfield, Mrs Chorley, Mrs.

Exley, Miss L. Hebblethwaite, Messrs F.W. Fison, G. Fison, R. Moore and Dr. Lewer.
Such a list is a fair indication of the influential members of Church and Village Society at the time.

The February issue includes a list of Church services which is then repeated each month:

Sundays	8 a.m. and 11.30 a.m. Communion
	10.30 a.m. Morning Prayer (and Litany on 2nd and 4th Sundays)
	6 p.m. Evening Prayer with sermon
Holy Days	11 a.m. Morning Prayer 11.30 a.m. Communion
	4 p.m. Evening Prayer
Ash Wednesday	7.30 a.m. and 11 a.m. Communion
	(plus Morning Prayer and Litany at 11 a.m.)
	7.30 p.m. Evening Prayer.
Weekdays	Wednesday and Friday 11 a.m. Morning Prayer and Litany
	Wednesday 7.30 p.m. Evening Prayer.
Occasional Offices	Baptisms Sunday 3 p.m. or Wednesday 7.30 p.m.
	Weddings by special arrangement.

A memorial of Archbishop Temple[52] just deceased was included in the February edition:

Archbishop Frederick Temple

We have been hearing and thinking much of late of that great man, Archbishop Temple, whose long term of earthly service for God and God's Church came to a close on December 23rd, 1902. Some of us may like to be reminded of his visit to Burley, more than thirty years ago, when he came to stay for a few days with his friend Mr. W. E. Forster, and to take part in certain educational meetings in the district. We may like to be reminded how the Bishop (it was in the early years of his Exeter episcopate) threw himself into the life of the place; how he visited the

59

mill and mill school; how he worshipped with us in church,
morning and evening, insisting on going and returning on foot
through the pouring rain, and how he afterwards expressed his
pleasure at the heartiness of our service. There may be some of
us, too, who still recall his preaching to us in the evening of
Sunday, Oct. 1st, 1871, his reading of the prayer for Unity be-
fore he   began his sermon, then his plain setting forth the story
of the rich young ruler (Mark x. 21) and his stirring character-
istic call to all there present to follow Christ.

The formation of the Parochial Church Council (PCC) looms large in the
magazines of March and April, culminating in the formal election at the
Annual Vestry meeting on 17th April. Members were to be chosen from the
sidesmen by the electors, namely the Vicar and his two churchwardens,
Arthur Greenwood and Robert Fox. The new PCC was to consist then of
the Vicar and his churchwardens and Messrs R. Gossop, R.W. Fox,
Hustwick, E.P. Arnold-Forster, J. Lake, W.T. Butterfield, G. Leach, F.
Leach, J. Exley, J. Painter, C. Wilkinson, S. Crabtree, W. Newbould, J.
Walls, W.H. Hannam, J. Hodgson, H. Mann, & G. Ogden. As Ruridecanal
Representatives, W.H. Mitchell and F.G. Fison were elected. Richard
Gossop (headteacher of the National School) was elected PCC secretary.
At the Vestry Meeting it was also agreed to hold Special Collections for
Home Missions, Foreign Missions, The Choir, Sunday School, Diocesan
Societies, Hospitals, Society for the conversion of Jews, and the
Elementary Teachers' Benevolent Society.

During the summer months various organisations held outdoor events
which were reported in the magazines. The Mothers met at Wharfeside,
and the Girls' Friendly Society met in the National School when rain
dashed the hopes of an outside event at Cathedine. Garden Teas took place
at Walton House (now the home of Ghyll Royd School) and at Highlands
in Moor Lane (now demolished). Further afield the Choir Boys had a good
day in Scarborough and the Choir Men went by train to Morecambe taking
their own gramophone for musical entertainment in the booked saloon
carriage.

In August the notes also record the arrival in Church of a new Brass Eagle Lectern, a gift of Sir Malby Crofton and Mrs. Yorke, in memory of their mother [Sophie Crofton]. The inscription included the dates 22nd September 1835 to 23rd July 1902. The Vicar adds:

The reason for the use of the eagle as the lectern is not altogether certain. Possibly, as some think, it is because the eagle is the emblem of St. John the Divine, and this would give it a symbolical meaning of a satisfactory kind. But be this as it may, the beauty of our new lectern is its own sufficient justification.

11. The 1903 Parish Magazine Cover
West Yorkshire Archives

The Vicar's notes in that month end with an appeal for an adjustable brass book rest for the pulpit, a lectern bible (revised version) and a new organ! November was the traditional month for the annual Church Bazaar for which stall holders worked for months ahead. There were 6 stalls for needlework, glass and china and several smaller stalls for sweets, dairy produce and postcards. Over the two days it was held at the Lecture Hall in 1903 a sum of £432 11s. was raised, a splendid result compared with the previous year's £14. A local poet, according to the Vicar (perhaps himself), had penned a verse in celebration, in the style of Edmund Spencer, :

> *A gallant wight there walked down Burley street*
> *Upon his arm did lean his lovesome wife;*
> *Y-dressed were they twain in costume meet*
> *Nor in their faces any look of strife*
> *But rather in their hearts was pleasure rife,*
> *For they were wending unto the Bazaar*
> *Where might be boughten things to gladden life;*
> *Nor shall their feet grow weary wending far*
> *Since close is now the Hall where store of good things are.*

In December the Vicar announced that from the following month the magazine would be different. 'Home Words' would replace 'Church Monthly', and it would be quarto size instead of octavo. Twenty four pages of quarto would give more space than the current magazine.

> *The front page also will present an entirely new appearance, it will be ornamental with a handsome ecclesiastical design printed in red and black, in place of the familiar, if somewhat inaccurate view of the Church. No advertisement will appear on the front page in future.*

During the succeeding year another project appeared and that was to have a new church in the village. It is not clear whether this was to be a second church or a replacement for St. Mary's. At this time the village was expanding in the vicinity of the Station and there were plans for an estate of imposing villas off Moor Lane opposite Scalebor. We know from John Lupton's diary that he was appointed a member of the committee to purchase the land for the new Church in 1904. He was asked to oversee the fencing of the land for grazing until the building work should commence. The field which had been bought was at the junction of Station Road and Langford Lane, where Rushy Beck Court now stands. The architects who were employed to draw up the plans were Connon and Chorley of Park

Place, Leeds. Harry Chorley was a member of the congregation, living at Moorville Cottage, at Woodhead. The plans were submitted in February 1906. They show a design on a much grander scale than St. Mary's. The new Church would have a square tower 72 feet tall, a nave and chancel

140 feet long and with two side aisles would be 76 feet wide. The windows were to be in perpendicular style with upper and lower lights. The east window was to be gothic in style with five lancet sections, the whole being 24 feet high. In the north east corner of the Church there was to be a basement containing a parochial meeting room, clergy and choir vestries, two W.Cs and a washroom. The main entrance to the Church was to be in the north west corner.

12. The 1910 Parish Magazine Cover
West Yorkshire Archives

In all the Church would have provided seating for 378 in the nave, 206 in the side aisles, 24 in a south side chapel and 28 in the Choir. Altogether 636 people could have been accommodated[53]. A building fund was

63

set up and features in the annual accounts, but in 1912 the sum amounted

to just over £66 and we assume that there was no major fund raising to complete the project. The First World War intervened and thoughts after that turned to maintaining and improving St. Mary's. The land itself remained as Church property for about fifty years and was sold in 1953.

In the first decade of the 20th Century, Mr. Buckley kept up his scholarly studies and one of his concerns was the 'problem of the Synoptic Gospels'. Briefly put this is the concern by students of the origin and writing of the three New Testament gospels of Matthew, Mark and Luke.

13. Rev.E.R. Buckley, M.A. photograph by kind permission of the Vicar and Churchwardens of Kirtlington Parish Church, Oxford.

In 1912 his book *Introduction to the Synoptic Problem* was published in London by Edward Arnold. He also had an interest in nineteenth century French History which later led him to publish two further books. From time to time he had the assistance of a curate, so that he would be able to divest himself of some of the parochial responsibilities in order to pursue his research. In 1910 his curate was Rev. D.S. Gillmore, M.A. and in 1914, Rev. S. R. Tomlinson, B.Sc. There was some continuity among the staff of the Parish. John Lupton remained Parish Clerk until 1910, when he was replaced by Mr. J. Painter. George Vine was the Verger through most of his incumbency. The organist, Mr. F.J. P. Drake, remained in post throughout Mr. Buckley's time. The church wardens changed, but Robert Fox, People's Warden, who had been elected to that post in 1869, continued to his retirement in 1909, when he was replaced by J. Exley. Three men particularly served in the role of Vicar's Warden during Eric Buckley's time, Arthur Greenwood of Greenholme, 1903-1909, Edward P. Arnold-Forster of Cathedine, 1910-1912 and Fred. D. Moore of Cathedine, 1913-19. These were men of substance and managerial experience in the village who would no doubt give the Vicar considerable help in running the Parish. Before Eric Buckley left Burley, Fred Vine became Vicar's Warden in 1920 and was to continue in that office until 1932.

This all suggests that there was a fair amount of stability in Church affairs despite the turmoil of the First World War which saw many men volunteering and conscripted into the armed forces. The main employer in the village, Wm. Fison and Co. of Greenholme Mills, would be able to provide employment for men and women of working age who were not caught up in the forces, as the books were full of orders for uniforms. There was inevitably much sadness as the list of those killed or maimed in the battles in northern France increased. The Vicar's own son, Humphrey Paul Kenneth Buckley, a Captain in the East Yorkshire Regiment, was killed in 1917 and is buried at Arras. His name is of course on the list of those who died in the conflict, on the north wall of St. Mary's.

The minutes of the PCC for 1920 give us some sense of the Parish life in Eric Buckley's last year as incumbent. Changes were afoot as the Parish was now part of the new Bradford Diocese created in 1919. The Vicar's Warden, Fred. D. Moore, played a key role as Chairman of the Finance Committee during the setting up of the Diocese[54]. The P.C.C. which had operated from 1903 at the instigation of the Vicar (see above) was now a legally constituted body under legislation agreed in 1919. Parliament that year agreed to the measures to create a new Church Assembly of bishops, clergy and laity and opened the way to more lay participation in Church of England government at national, diocesan, deanery and parish levels.

The minutes of the first legally held meeting in September 1920, indicate that the Vicar was in the chair. The minutes are not entirely clear, but presumably there had been a Vestry meeting at which the Vicar had explained the new enabling Bill which gave powers to a PCC for the first time. With 918 persons on the Parish Electoral Roll, it was agreed to have ten members on the council. Fourteen were nominated and those elected were:

Miss F. Arnold-Forster, Miss J. Dixon, Mr. W. Crabtree, Mr. J. Exley (Vicar's Warden), Mr. R. Gossop, Mr. S. Mann, Mr. W. Newbould, Mr. J.W. Simpson, Mr. W. Freer Thonger, and Mr. F. Vine (People's Warden). Richard Gossop (Head of Burley National School) was elected Secretary and Treasurer.

The PCC passed two resolutions at the first meeting. They voted to have:
    'some voice in the appointment of new incumbents' and
    'some voice before sweeping changes were made in the nature of
      services'.
It is interesting to reflect that the Vicar had reordered the services soon after his arrival in 1902, and perhaps long memories led to the second resolution. The first possibly indicates that some of the PCC members were already aware that Mr. Buckley was looking elsewhere for a living. They wanted to make sure that they had some say in the choice of his successor and not to leave it entirely in the hands of the patron. The patronage at this time was in the hands of the Trustees of Mrs Sophia Crofton, deceased, of Burley Hall.

At the PCC meeting in Dec 1920, the old problem of finance came up, and the minutes acknowledge the 'seriousness of the position' at the same time as 'detailing absolutely necessary repairs of the Church'. The question of how to deal with them was left over to another meeting though an appeal for funds was to be made. The building of another church was clearly impossible. An appeal had raised £315 by the time of the Annual Vestry Meeting in the Spring of 1921 and the first AGM of the PCC. The Wardens were reappointed and the PCC was reelected en bloc. The Vicar was absent from this meeting which would have been the last before he left

Burley for his next appointment. In September the minutes of the PCC note that Miss Frances Arnold-Forster had died, the last of the children adopted by William and Jane Forster in 1859, who had been a devoted member of the Church.

Rev Eric R. Buckley was appointed the Rector of Polstead in Essex in 1921 and thereafter Archdeacon of Sudbury in 1930 and Archdeacon of Ipswich in 1932. He retired to Colchester in 1945 and died in 1948. His obituary notes that he was a lover of cricket as well as being a reputable historian and theologian.

CHAPTER FOUR

THE INTERWAR YEARS

The wisdom of our fathers under the good hand of God gave to the Church of England the Book of Common Prayer in English Speech. It is, and we believe always will be, one of the great books of the world...Since 1662 there has been change almost beyond belief...

The preface to the 1928 Prayer Book.

It is not clear that the PCC had any representation in the appointment of the next Vicar, **William Crawford Allan**, but he was instituted in April 1922. He was born in 1866, in Scotland, and graduated from the University of Glasgow with an M.A. in 1888, and subsequently with a Bachelor of Divinity from the University of Edinburgh in 1890. He served as curate in Richmond (Yorkshire), Keighley and Bradford, before moving to Leeds, where he served in Wortley and then as perpetual curate in Stourton from 1906 to 1921. Unfortunately we have little personal information about him and his circumstances. The 1911 Census shows that he was living in Leeds and was a widower, but parishioners in Burley who have personal memories of him, remember his second wife. We are relying on PCC minutes and other parish records. Minutes reveal key decisions and some of the discussions which took place, as interpreted by the Secretary and subject to agreement by the members. Fortunately for the historian the PCC secretary was the National School Headteacher, who seems to have written a reasonably full coverage of meetings.

The new Vicar's first annual meeting of parishioners was in 1922, when his churchwardens were J. Exley and F. Vine, who were continuing in office from previous years. He was immediately faced with the need for repairs to the Church and its fabric. An estimate for the cost of repairing the spire came to £70. The interior needed redecorating and the pews and choir stalls renovating. The gas light fittings had to be replaced and it was considered that electric power and lighting were the answer. Heating in the Chancel was not adequate, either, and it was agreed to spend £35 on that. Not for the first time the need to increase Church income became a subject for debate, and it was decided to implement a Free Will Offering scheme in June 1923. The first estimate of income from the Scheme suggested it would reach £300 if all promises were met. As with later schemes the amount collected did not live up to expectations but in general proved a very useful means of meeting Church expenses.

Bradford Diocese needed financial support and introduced the system of Parochial Quotas in the 1920s. The PCC each year from this time has had to find the amounts requested. In 1926 the quota requested was £80 and it rose to £94 in 1929 which was paid in full. This represented 17 percent of the Parish's total expenditure in 1929. The financial statement for that year shows that the main sources of income were ordinary collections in services (£158), freewill offerings (£170) and a Sale of Work (£130) in a total income of £558. On the expenditure side the main items were wages for the Verger, Sexton and Parish Clerk (£162), Organist and Choir (£78), Heating and Lighting (£34) and Church and Vicarage repairs (£45). Grants and Special Collections were made and given to various groups and causes including the Sunday School, Missionary Societies, the National Society, Miners' Relief Fund, Earl Haig's Fund and Hospitals, amounting to £41. The finances were supported by a Bank Overdraft of £18. It has to be noted that this was a period of economic and financial difficulty in the country and in the developed world. The PCC would be faced with considerable difficulty in meeting all needs. There is no doubt from the minutes that hard choices had to be made. Inevitably the Diocesan Quota was always a subject of some concern. As ever various rescue bids were made to help church finances. Annual sales of work before Christmas in the 1930s, raised considerable sums, for example in 1932, £326, and in 1934, £360.

Other far-reaching issues were being considered in PCC meetings in Burley and elsewhere in Crawford Allan's time. The extent to which the State should be able to influence Church decisions was brought to a head in 1927 when a revised 1662 Prayer Book failed to reach a sufficient majority in the House of Commons for it to be presented for Royal assent. The Book which had been prepared by the Anglican Church hierarchy had been accepted by the Church Assembly, both the Convocations of York and Canterbury and the House of Lords. The amended version of 1928 suffered the same fate. An alternative version of the Communion Service had caused the greatest discord with its provision for the reservation of the sacrament. The opposition in the country came from those who feared the new measure was too Catholic in its approach, stressing the sacramental rather the commemorative aspect of the Eucharist. Despite this and the opposition in the House of Commons, many Bishops approved its use in part. In Burley the PCC agreed in July 1929 that the new 1928 Book could be used except 'the new Canon of Communion and the Reservation of the Sacrament', a view that was reiterated when the time came in 1936 for a new Vicar to be appointed. It was stipulated then that 'the PCC would like a broad churchman to be appointed as Vicar, one who would, in celebrating the sacrament, use the form of consecration prescribed in the 1662 Prayer Book and would not practise reservation'. Meanwhile as in many broad churches some parts of the 1928 Book were used and came to be widely accepted, for example the shortened form of the Commandments from the New Testament.

New Archbishops had been installed in 1929, Cosmo Lang in Canterbury and William Temple in York, and their first message to the Church was to encourage spiritual renewal of the clergy and the people. They issued a pastoral letter to be read in all churches in July 1929. In it they referred to the dispute over the 1928 Revised Prayer Book:

> *Here may we speak a word about the difficulties in the ordering of our Common Prayer which recent events have brought about....Suffice it then to say that the true way of solving these difficulties is that men of different outlook and traditions should not only tolerate but learn from one another, should come to-gether, study together, so that all may bring whatever truth or experience they severally prize as an offering for the enrichment of the whole Church...*[55].

70

The minutes also record attempts by some members of the PCC to reinvigorate the services at St. Mary's by the introduction of a more up to date hymn book to replace the *Ancient and Modern* then in use. The *English Hymnal* published in 1906 with Ralph Vaughan Williams as its editor was suggested by Mr. C. Hannam in 1926. He criticised *Ancient and Modern* for its high pitched tunes, many poor tunes and its sentimental words. This view had been expressed in the preface to the *English Hymnal* when it was first published. Twelve copies of this hymn book were bought for perusal but no further action seems to have been taken. Nearly ten years later in 1935, the Vicar also argued for new hymn books, this time advocating *Songs of Praise* which had been published in 1925 and had quickly become used in many schools. On finding out that new books for the choir and congregation would cost £32, the matter was again deferred.

During the 1930s several long serving members of the Church during Crawford Allan's incumbency retired or died. Richard Gossop who had been PCC secretary for 14 years, and a member of the Choir, retired from his Church commitments. After retiring from his post as Headteacher of the National School, he continued to sit on the Burley Urban District Council of which he had been Chairman in 1932. Fred Vine who was People's Warden from 1920 died in 1932. E.G.H. Mitchell retired from the position of Vicar's Warden after six years in 1931, and was replaced by Harry Chorley for the rest Allan's time.

William Crawford Allan gave up his living in 1935. At a ceremony to mark his departure, chaired by Dr. Gilmour, the Superintendent at Scalebor Hospital, a member of the PCC, Harry Chorley, Vicar's Warden, presented the Vicar with a gift of £100. Various farewell speeches were made including one by Rev. W. Brown Tucker, representing the Free Churches, a pleasing sign of growing ecumenism in the Village. There is no record of the Catholic priest, Father LeFevre, from the newly built Church of Saints John Fisher and Thomas More, being present.

A priedieu, now standing next to the pulpit, was given to the Church in memory of his service to the Parish. He retired to Abingdon in Berkshire at

71

the age of 60.

He was succeeded by **Rev Edmund Neville Pedley.** The new vicar was instituted and inducted to St. Mary's by the Bishop of Bradford, Dr. A.W.F. Blunt, in October 1936. The Bishop's Chaplain was one of the Vicar's brothers. Neville Pedley was born in Morley in 1890, the son of Rev. George Pedley. He graduated from Queen's College Cambridge, in 1915 and was ordained Deacon that year and Priest in 1916. Prior to going to Cambridge, he spent some years as an elementary school teacher in Bradford. He became a Chaplain to the Forces in the First World War, and remained an Honorary Chaplain until 1920. His first curacy was at All Saints Parish Church in Little Horton Bradford, from which he moved in 1926 to be Vicar of Ingrow, in Keighley, where he spent ten years. In his approach to the parishioners he seemed 'a broad churchman with a light touch' as one of them informed us. He was very musical and enjoyed social occasions like the annual Shrove Tuesday gatherings. Some of those who still remember him were also were struck by the fact that he owned a Jaguar car, not normally in those days associated with Vicars.

Up to the beginning of the Second World War in 1939, Rev Pedley was assisted by Harry Chorley followed by Dr. Garscadden as Vicar's wardens, and William Newbould as the People's warden. The PCC consisted of twelve members most of whom had served for several years previously. The new Vicar, like his predecessor, was faced with expensive repairs needed in the Church. He had been fortunate to move into a Vicarage that had been refurbished with new fireplaces, bathrooms, sinks, and new electric wiring. The total cost of the repairs had come to £680 but some of that money still needed to be found. The state of the Church was also causing concern, so much so that the Vicar is reported to have spoken out about it at the Annual Parochial Meeting in 1937. He said 'it nearly amounts to blasphemy to call it a church'…and further, 'I hope one day we shall have a church of which we may be proud'[56].

An appeal for funds to do the necessary renovations was launched and a hoped for increase in Free Will Offerings was requested. A new member

Group taken at the opening of Burley Church Garden Party at "Cathedine," on July 24th. Left to right: Front row—Mrs. Peter Douty, Mrs. J. G. Hutchinson, Mrs. Maufe, Lady Whitehead (who performed the opening ceremony), Mrs. Pedley. Back row—Col. F. W. B. Maufe, Mr. W. Newbould (churchwarden), Rev. E. N. Pedley, Mrs. Frank Pepper, Mr. G. H. Pepper.

14. A garden party at Cathedine. Wharfedale Newspapers, 1937.

of the PCC in 1937, Eric Maufe, (a member of the Muff family, of the famous department store in Bradford, Brown and Muffs) recommended that the Church should realise the money that was tied up in the land bought in 1904 as a site for a new Church. That was not now regarded as a feasible project, but the land was not sold at this time. Other monies were used and in August 1938 the local press reported that 'the organ was being overhauled. Two small lancet windows were built on either side of the sanctuary to provide more light. The porch and vestry were to receive attention and also the exterior of the building and the churchyard'[57].

Once essential repairs had been completed the PCC could turn its attention to future improvements. Since Neville Pedley's arrival the church congregation and particularly the number of communicants had increased. The electoral roll still stood at a healthy 612 in 1938 and the accounts were said to be in a creditable state. Thus in 1938 it was agreed to seek a faculty to enlarge the vestry at the west end of the church. The following year the Vicar suggested that changes might be made in the furniture of the

15. Group of St. Mary's congregation at the Annual Bazaar in 1937. The Vicar, Rev. Neville Pedley is third from the left at the back. (Wharfedale Newspapers)

sanctuary, to include a reredos, a new altar, new panelling and altar rails. Such developments, he thought, could be paid for by the Free Will Offering and gift days, replacing the annual November bazaar, which he thought relied too heavily on raffles. Garden parties, however, continued to be held. Gifts to Missionary Societies, such as CMS, SPG, the National Society and Waifs and Strays, continued to be given each year though the proportion of church income donated fell below the levels of the late nineteenth century. In 1928 the amount given was £35 from a total income of £576.

During this inter-war period many changes were occurring both in Burley and in the country more widely. The mills that had provided so much employment for many residents and their families saw their markets declining and this caused periods of unemployment. For the owners and managers there was continuing uncertainty. There was social unrest, inequality and demands for change, not least from the Labour movement. A world financial crisis in 1929 and in the early 1930s saw similar problems throughout the industrialised countries. Another source of great concern was the rise of fascism particularly in Germany, Spain, Italy and

Japan leading to threats of war. In the Anglican Church, the recognition of the need for a Christian response to these problems was promoted by the Archbishop of York, William Temple.

The Second World War put a stop to plans for further changes in the fabric of St. Mary's. The PCC had to buy black out material for the windows so that the normally well attended Evensong could continue at 6 p.m. Plans for any emergencies and fire watching had to be made. The Verger was to be on hand to unlock the Church if an air raid warning was sounded. The PCC switched its accounts from deposits at the village branch of Martin's Bank to Government War Stock. Special collections were made for Forces' benevolent funds. The Church came up to its centenary in the middle of the War. Celebrations were muted however, as the date coincided with the 'Wings for Victory' nationwide savings week to help the war effort. Rev Eric Buckley, then Archdeacon of Ipswich, was invited to preach at a special service to mark the centenary on 20th June 1943.

An innovation in the pattern of services occurred during the War when Choral Communion was celebrated on the first Sunday of each month. At this time communion wafers were introduced, in place of pieces of whole meal bread 'which were somewhat difficult to masticate'[58]. This was said to be just for the duration of the War, but in fact seems to have been adopted ever since. The general rubrick of the administration of Holy Communion in the 1928 Prayer Book in any case allowed this. *"It is desirable that the Bread shall be the best and purest wheat bread, whether loaf or*

16. 1930 St. Mary's interior with pulpit on the north side and a World War I memorial on the south of the chancel. S.Gunton.

wafer that conveniently may be gotten "[59]. The choir at this time was still popular with boys and there were often ten or a dozen of them singing treble at Morning and Evening Services as well as at Choral Communion. The other parts were sung mainly by men, though at least one parishioner at that time remembers a group of ladies singing the alto part. They were rehearsed by the Vicar and sat in the front pew in the nave.

During the War the names of those serving in the Forces were read out once a month, and deaths were recorded. Several long serving members of the Church died naturally during the War years, including William Newbould and Harry Chorley. Miss Dixon and Mr. W. H Vine completed 50 years service and in particular their membership and help with the Church choir was noted in the PCC Minutes of 1942. As the War was drawing to an end in 1945 the Vicar appealed to those present at the Annual Vestry and Parochial Meeting in March

> *for sympathy and understanding to those who would soon be returning from war service. They would be more mature and better fitted to lead and people at home would have to try and see things through their eyes. Young people must be afforded opportunities of leadership and service, directly through the church and indirectly for the community, and above all they must be made to feel that they were needed*[60].

CHAPTER FIVE
THE POST-WAR YEARS, 1945 – 1969

The suffering caused by existing evils makes a claim upon our sympathy which the Christian heart and conscience cannot ignore...Society must be so arranged as to give to every citizen the maximum opportunity for making deliberate choices and the best possible training for the use of that opportunity...Every child should have the opportunity of an education till years of maturity, so planned as to allow for their peculiar aptitudes and make possible their full development. This education should throughout be inspired by faith in God and find its focus in worship. William Temple[61].

The Second World War ended in August 1945 when hostilities in the Far East ceased, three months after the end of the war in Europe. Great social changes were planned for peace time, in order to try to remove the social inequalities which had become painfully obvious in pre-war Britain. One of the outstanding pieces of legislation enacted in war time, which was to have a far-reaching effect on Burley and the country more widely, was the Education Act of 1944. All-age elementary schools, like Burley's National School and the Main Street Council School, were to be abolished and replaced so that all children would have primary education to 11 years and seconday education in separate schools from 11 years onwards.

Further there was to be a reclassification of Church schools. They could choose whether to be Aided or Controlled. Aided schools were to receive grants to pay teachers' salaries and other maintenance charges, and a grant of 50% towards the cost of alteration to buildings, the cost of all internal repairs and half the cost of external repairs. The Church would have to fund the rest. Appointment of staff remained in control of the Managers, the majority of whom were to be nominated by the Church. This had been roughly how the National School had operated before the War. Controlled schools were to have managers, the majority of whom would be appointed by the local education authority (LEA), but with the rest being Church representatives. The staff would be appointed by the LEA but the Church had the right to appoint a teacher of religious education. The schools were then totally funded by the LEA.

The alternatives for the future of the National School were discussed at length by the PCC in 1945 and 1946. How much control did St. Mary's PCC wish to have over their school in the future? The cost implications of more control were fully considered. After surveys of the premises, which showed the need for a permanent stage, two new classrooms and new lavatories, it was indicated that the Church would have to find £15,500. The PCC decided to take on the challenge and asked that the school be designated as Aided.

Four years later when the West Riding Education Authority implemented the Act making the transition to primary and secondary education in April 1950, the PCC bowed to the inevitable and accepted the less financially demanding Controlled status. This was after convincing arguments by one of its members, David Nealy, a master at Prince Henry's Grammar School in Otley. Main Street Council School closed and virtually all children of primary age in Burley then came to the new Burley Controlled Church of England Junior Mixed and Infants School in the Aireville Terrace premises of the former National School. Some however made the trek up to Burley Woodhead Primary school, a controlled school in the Menston parish. Those over 11 years of age went to the new Secondary Modern School at Ben Rhydding, or if they had passed the 11 plus examination, to one of the local Grammar Schools. The feelings which had caused the split in the village in 1898 had now largely disappeared, and there was a stronger ecumenical sense in education. An Agreed Syllabus of Religious Education, approved by representatives of the Churches and the West Riding, was the basis of teaching from then onwards. Each day began with a corporate act of worship as the 1944 Act stipulated.

The Vicar remained Chairman of the School Managers, but his powers and responsibilities were now much reduced from those exercised by his predecessors. Albert Simmons who became Headteacher of the National

School in 1937, and also Secretary to the PCC, became the Head of the new primary school. The PCC could nominate parishioners to be Foundation managers of the School and F.W.B. Maufe continued in office having been first appointed as a manager of the National School in 1946.

The membership of the PCC was slowly changing. A new member who had first been elected to the Council in 1942 was James Verdi (Jim) Slater, and he became Vicar's Warden in the first post war PCC in 1946. A bank manager with experience as an Urban District Councillor, Jim was to serve as Church Warden for many years. John Rayner, who later became a lay reader and leader of the Youth Fellowship, was elected to the PCC in 1947 and became People's Warden for two years in 1950. F.W.B.(Eric) Maufe was elected People's Warden in his place in 1952 and remained a Warden until 1966. Among the women who gave long service were the Vicar's wife, Mrs Pedley, Miss Rogers, Miss Horton and Miss Dean, who was a Sunday School teacher for many years. Raymond Gill and James Turnbull, both young men who were keen members of the Youth Fellowship, were elected to the PCC in the early 1950s.

The St.Mary's Youth Fellowship was formed in April 1947 for young people over 14 years. Members met in the Parish Room and later, when the group had been affiliated to the West Riding Youth Organisation, they were allowed to meet in the Aireville Terrace School. On Tuesday and Thursday evenings, the members, numbering 20 to 30, met for drama and dancing as well as discussions about current affairs, religion and hobbies. It was expected that they would attend services on Sunday, usually even-song. There were occasional quiz nights, films and visits to other Youth Clubs. In 1951 and 1954 the members were taken on visits to Germany arranged by John Rayner. Membership for the young men was interrupted by the calls of National Service, generally lasting two years from the age of 18.

Attention to the Church fabric, which had been out of the question during the War years, again seemed necessary and possible. At the Vicar's suggestion a recording of a peal of bells was installed in the tower. 'It was agreed to raise the money by an appeal'[62].The interior of the Church was redecorated, the organ overhauled and a piano purchased. An aperture was made in the west wall above the door so that films could be projected into the nave. The Vicar's son was keen to act as projectionist and a selection of films was hired for showing. At last the Vicar's suggestion for refurnishing the sanctuary and chancel, made in 1939, was realised. A faculty was obtained for a new altar, altar rails, choir and clergy stalls as well as a new repositioned pulpit. These were made in English oak at the workshops of Robert Thompson 'the mouseman' at Kilburn, and fitted in 1952 at a total cost of £1100. The reredos which Neville Pedley wanted was not included at this time. Money to pay Robert Thompson Craftsmen Ltd. came from Church funds, a Gift Day and a Garden Party in 1952. The old furnishings were taken to a Bradford Church.

Apart from local Church needs the Diocese was making increasing calls on Parishes for support.

> ..In April 1945, Bishop Blunt launched the Forward Movement
> Appeal, setting a target of £200,000. ...The need was for new
> church buildings, clergy stipends, new vicarages, improvements
> to schools, training for teachers and clergy, moral welfare and
> youth work[63].

The regular Diocesan Quota had to be found on top of any gifts to the Forward Movement Appeal. An envelope scheme had been started in 1949 to encourage regular giving, but the Warden and Treasurer, Jim Slater, commented that the numbers participating were never large enough and the offertory was disappointing. Out of an electoral roll of over 500 only 85 parishioners were regular contributors to the envelope scheme. Income relied on Gift Days in the late 1940s when as much as £270 could be donated. Bazaars were often better for fund raising but relied on a lot of effort by a few willing souls. In 1949 the Annual Bazaar raised £950 and in 1952, £750. The land at the junction of Langford Lane and Station Road, once purchased as a site for a new Church, was at last sold for £600 in 1953. From these sources small gifts were given each year to Missionary Societies and other charities.

1953 was the year of the coronation of Queen Elizabeth II. The village celebrated the event with a procession and various social events in the Lecture Hall, which afterwards was renamed the Queen's Hall. The Church gave Coronation Prayer Books to Sunday School scholars and put on floral displays in the approach path, the nave and chancel. Unfortunately the day of the Coronation in June was one of miserable cool weather which dampened the spirit of rejoicing considerably.

17. Rev. Neville Pedley, M.A.
By permission of
Rev. J. Turnbull

One of the outcomes of the increased subvention to the Diocese was that the Vicar benefitted. His salary was increased to the minimum recommended £500. The curacy fund was dormant at this stage, even though Neville Pedley from time to time requested the help of an assistant curate. He was made Rural Dean of Otley in 1950 which gave him extra responsibilities and a greater time commitment. In his final year as Vicar of St. Mary's, he again raised the idea of having a curate, because his health was not good, and as well as all his other work, he was looking after choir rehearsals. The PCC discussed the question, but had no solution. The Vicar acknowledged that 'there was a great shortage of men willing to work in the Northern Province'[64]. Continuing ill health led to Neville Pedley resigning the incumbency at the end of 1954 aged 64. He and his wife moved from the Vicarage to Menston . He came back to celebrate the 50th anniversary of his priesting in 1966, but sadly died in 1968, his funeral being held at St. Mary's.

Before the next incumbent was named, the PCC discussed the question of how he should be appointed. It seems to have been the case that the patronage, traditionally exercised by the owner of Burley Hall, had not been transferred by the executors of the late Lionel Cresswell, to Percy

Dalton, when the Hall had been sold to him in the 1930s. The executors, it transpired, were intending to pass on the advowson (the right of patronage) to the Bishop of Bradford. A motion of protest was sent to the executors by the PCC expressing their desire that the patronage should stay in private hands, and that the traditional right of four members of the PCC to be consulted about the appointment should be maintained. [The legal position was not finally clarified until 1966.] The patrons acted quickly to have another priest appointed and the Wardens were able to announce that the Rev. John Beardsmore, assistant curate in Otley, had accepted the position, with the proviso that he could also be the Chaplain of Scalebor Park Hospital[65].

Rev. John Beardsmore, was instituted and inducted to the Parish on 1st April 1955. John was born in 1919 and was a member of the armed forces during World War II, reaching the rank of major. Part of his service was in India. He entered Kelham theological college[66] in 1946 and was ordained priest in 1951 at Lichfield Cathedral. After being assistant curate in Walsall from 1951 to 1953, he was invited to Otley Parish Church for his second curacy. The churchwardens were obviously pleased to have a man with a wife and young family of three, who did not have to move very far.

John's first action was to note that it was soon to be the centenary of the creation of St. Mary's parish and suggested an Evangelistic Mission to take place during 1956. A sermon in February by the Bishop of Knaresborough was designed to stimulate discussion about all aspects of parochial life. At the Annual Vestry and Parochial meeting in March, the Vicar outlined the need for extra income to be found for updating the fabric, the heating, the lighting and cleaning of the Church. The Mission hopefully would increase participation in all congregational activities. There was already a good basis for this in the number of existing organisations. These included Sunday School, Youth Fellowship, Young Wives Group, Mothers' Union, Senior Fellowship and St. Mary's Players. The Churchwardens, Jim Slater and Eric Maufe, backed up the Vicar, pointing out that they hoped men would be willing to consider taking on roles as sidesmen and even being "trainees" for the position of warden.

Rev K. Stapleton from Holbeck was invited to lead the Mission in the autumn.

Out of the discussions during the Mission, several proposals were made, some of which were eventually realised and noted in the PCC meetings of 1956 and 1957. A Garden of Rest for Ashes was created on the eastern side of the Church. Lighting in the Church was improved. New robes for the Choir (under the leadership of Mr. & Mrs White) were made by Miss Rogers and the Choir rejoined the Royal School of Church Music. More people offered themselves for confirmation and thirty adults were confirmed in 1957. The possibility of having a new Vestry was raised again, though nothing was done. A family service was suggested as an addition to the Sunday services, and training some youths as Altar Servers was proposed. The Vicar declined to act on these last two ideas, however.

Increased giving to the Church was very much on the minds of the Vicar and Wardens. There were 400 people on the Electoral Roll and 'if they gave one shilling per week, our housekeeping money problem would be solved' said the Vicar[67]. Money from the contingency account had been used for extensive work which had been necessary for the renovation, replastering and redecoration in the Church. The Parish Room needed major repairs and the rent income was not sufficient to fund them. Various money raising schemes were again suggested by the PCC and provided temporary reprieve. A Gift Day in 1958 raised £475 and a Spring Fayre the following year £440.

A more radical approach to Church giving was being adopted at this time in many parishes in the country known as Christian Stewardship. A brochure produced by St. Mary's gave the background to it. 'The seeds of our campaign were sown at the Lambeth Conference in 1958. As Anglicans we were then charged with the duty of Christian Stewardship which is defined as the regarding of ourselves – our time, our talents and our money – as a trust from God to be utilised in His service. This charge was enthusiastically accepted by our own Diocese in June 1959'[68]. After several discussions in the PCC an open meeting was held to acquaint parishioners with the ideas behind the Stewardship Campaign. Church warden Eric Maufe took the chair of the campaign and, to inaugurate it, a dinner was held at the Craiglands Hotel in Ilkley, in February 1962. Invitations were given to electoral roll members and other likely participants . A cottage in Main Street, loaned by the Daltons, became the Stewardship Office. A target of £3000 per annum was thought possible and several committees were set up to supervise the time and talents aspect.

In the first year £5000 was realised and by the end of the year the Vicar was able to consider the appointment of a curate. Further the Diocesan quota was paid in full, and extra allocations were made to Parish organisations and Missions. Eric Maufe thanked everyone for the efforts that had been made but went on to say 'there is more to Christian Stewardship than putting gifts in envelopes. There are some needs which can only be met by personal service – the giving of time and effort.' He listed nine projects which needed support:
1. A team for visiting children on their birthdays if they had been baptised in Church.
2. Four more Sunday School teachers.
3. Ten Sunday School assistants to the teachers.
4. Several men and women to form a rota to act as hosts and hostesses at Youth Meetings after Church on Sundays.
5. Five men and five women to undertake visiting as recommended by the Vicar.
6. Any number of younger or youthful people to come to God's Acre on Wednesday evenings during the summer – to enjoy themselves with rake, saw, spade, shears etc.
7. Three ladies to accept the task of looking after the choir robes and cassocks.
8. Reinforcements for the choir – in fact, we need reinforcements for all our teams from time to time.
9. Several car owners who would collect, on their own way to Church, someone who can no longer make the journey on foot.
The Vicar hoped that the campaign would put the Parish finances on a

sound basis 'so avoiding the unworthy paraphernalia of Bazaars, Bring and Buy, Jumble Sales and so forth'[69].

Many of these projects were well supported. Christian Stewardship became an accepted part of Parish life, and though there have been times of doubt and concern about the level of giving, it has remained a key strategy of the Church. In 1961 out of church expenditure totalling £2200 only £89 had been donated to missions and other charities. By 1968 however a much greater proportion of the income was given, £550 out of £3836.

Youth work continued to be an important part of the St Mary's mission. John Rayner who had led the Youth Fellowship for 14 years up to 1961, retired and was replaced by Raymond Gill. Meetings were held in the Aireville Terrace school on Thursday evenings and in the Parish Room on Sunday evenings. An influential Government report on Youth Work throughout the country, the Albemarle Report, was published in 1961. This recommended among other things that Local Authorities should take more action in providing services to youth and the training and payment of Youth Leaders. It was possible for the Parish Youth Fellowship, through its affiliation to the West Riding Youth Service to benefit from training and joint events across the County. The Fellowship was successful for several years at Area and County Youth Drama Festivals. Margaret and Dennis Warwick helped Raymond Gill at this time and were supported by several very keen members and their parents. June Wellbourne, Carol Edwards, Winifred Clough, Angela Johnson, Peter Bennett, Andrew Horton, Tom Pickard and Alan Whitehead were among these.

After several problems had arisen as a consequence of using Primary School classrooms, the Vicar felt obliged to discontinue the use of the School by the Youth Fellowship during the week. Meanwhile, negotiations took place with the West Riding and a leader paid by the Local authority was appointed for one evening per week. The former Primitive Methodist Church in Sun Lane became vacant in the mid-sixties and Ilkley Urban District Council purchased the building for use as a Youth Club. In 1967 the West Riding took over the running of the Club and payment of its leaders. The management committee, under the chairmanship of Jim Shelton, had representatives from the Church, namely Sam Wheeler, Nigel Cottam and Jim Bennett. Raymond Gill resigned when new leaders were appointed.

Meanwhile changes had been taking place amongst those holding official positions in the Church. Albert Simmons retired in 1957 after over twenty years as Head of Aireville Terrace School. Frank Newbould, was appointed to replace him. The resignation of Albert Simmons entailed a change of Secretary of the PCC. Jim Bennett took on this role which he kept for twenty five years. David Nealy, a Lay Reader, who had also been a member of the PCC for about twenty years resigned in 1966. He had written his well-researched history of the Church, which was published as a pamphlet in 1960. John Rayner qualified as a Lay Reader and gave many years of service. The Vicar gained the support of an assistant Curate in 1965, when Rev Graham Betteridge took up residence in Burley. He moved on to be Priest in Charge at St. Hugh's in Baildon in September 1967. The long serving verger, Albert Vine, retired in 1968.

In 1960 the Vicar expressed his worries about the size of the Vicarage and the cost of its upkeep. White Rose Cottage on Main Street was considered as an alternative, but the price was thought to be too high. An agreed solution was to create a self-contained flat on the ground floor of the existing Vicarage. The PCC agreed to pay for a good proportion of the alteration costs (£850). The flat was let out to the first tenant, Mrs Kilby, in 1961. The cost of running God's Acre was also a problem, despite the volunteer helpers who kept the cemetery tidy during the summer months. Eventually after negotiations with Ilkley Urban District Council, it was agreed that as a public cemetery it should be maintained and controlled by a public body rather than the Church. It was handed over to Ilkley in 1967. This saved an annual expense of £90, which does not sound much but obviously helped the Church treasurer in balancing the books. [When Ilkley UDC was abolished under the Local Government Reform Act of 1972, the management of the cemetery passed to Bradford Metropolitan District Council in 1974.]

The interior of St. Mary's took on a number of new features in the 1960s during the incumbency of John Beardsmore. Thanks to a generous donation from the former residents of Burley Hall, Mr. & Mrs. Percy Dalton, new war memorials were placed on the north and south walls of the nave, the Maude tablet was brought from the porch on to the west wall, and a highly decorated triptych was placed behind the altar in 1960. The triptych caused much discussion in the PCC and a decision was delayed for a month for consultations. The reason for this was that the riddel posts, and the curtains hung on them around the altar, which had been part of the sanctuary furniture installed in 1952, had to be removed and several members of the congregation were not happy to see them go. There are probably still some older members of the congregation who would have preferred the curtains to the triptych. A further issue about furniture arose when the trustees of the Cresswell bequest announced that they wished to have a memorial for the former Lord of the Manor, Lionel Cresswell, placed in St. Mary's in 1966. £250 was donated, and the PCC decided to

DAY, APRIL 28th, 1967

The Bishop of Bradford, the Rt. Rev. Michael Parker conducted a service of confirmation at St. Mary's Parish Church, Burley-in-Wharfedale on Sunday afternoon. Left to right are: Mr. Albert Vine (verger), Mr. J. V. Slater (warden), Rev. John Beardsmore (Vicar), the Bishop, the Rev. Graham Betteridge (curate) and Mr. S. Wheeler (warden)

18. Visit of the Bishop of Bradford in 1967.   Wharfedale Newspapers.

have a wooden lectern produced in the Thompson workshops to match the rest of the sanctuary furniture. This was to replace the brass eagle lectern which had been donated to the Church in memory of Mrs Sophia Crofton, daughter of Thomas Horsfall, another former Lord of the Manor. Again there was dissent over the proposed change, but eventually the brass lectern was sold by agents in London to a church in West Africa, and the wooden lectern installed.

Some changes were being discussed in the liturgy and in ecumenical relations during John Beardsmore's time. A Prayer Book measure of 1965 allowed the Anglican Church lawfully to embark on Prayer Book reform without recourse to Parliament. The first revision, Series 1, was presented to the Church Assembly in 1966, and embodied many of the variations from the 1662 Prayer Book which were already in use. Series 2 was published in 1967 and provided alternative forms for Morning and Evening Prayer, Burial of the Dead, Churching and a draft for Holy Communion for experimental use. This draft was greeted with enthusiasm by the Church Assembly. The Peace became part of the service. The fourfold Eucharistic act of offertory, giving thanks, breaking, and distributing, obscured in the 1662 rite was now made explicit. There was the addition of an Old Testament reading, provision for the use of psalms and for flexibility in the forms of intercession.

There was much discussion about the institution of the Parish Communion as the appropriate form for the main service on Sundays and the use of Series 1. With the publication of Series 2 in 1967, however, and after an experimental period of using it at the end of the year, it was agreed that the Series 2 Communion service would be used once a month from March 1968. Readings from the New Testament were increasingly being drawn from the New English Bible, published in 1961. Archbishop Michael Ramsey had welcomed its publication.

> It is no exaggeration to say that it brings out the meaning of the story with a new vividness; it does this because the translators have achieved a new and scholarly grasp of what the Greek (or Hebrew) really means and have conveyed this to a degree

88

which their predecessors in English versions have often missed.... That New Bible is found to give fresh historical vividness to a whole narrative... It carries meaning across from ancient author to modern reader[70].

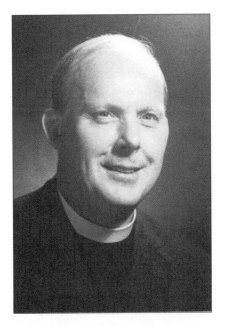

19. Rev John Beardsmore

Throughout society in the 1960s there was much desire for change. In 1964, a Labour government was elected for the first time since 1950, with Harold Wilson, a Yorkshireman, becoming Prime Minister and declaring that his government would create a 'classless dynamic new Britain' forged out of 'the white heat of new technology'. There were numerous radical political groups wanting even more change than Harold Wilson could offer. Among these were feminists who wished to remove the 'glass ceiling' which prevented women aspiring to positions of equality with men in work and society. As yet this had not had any effect on the Church of England, even though the influential Paul Report published in 1964 on the deployment of the Clergy revealed that the Church was short of manpower. At no point were women mentioned as possibly having the vocation to become deacons and priests. There were also serious theological debates and Bishop John Robinson's *Honest to God* published in 1963 by the SCM Press caused a great stir. He argued that much of the Gospel uses mythological language and an antiquated world-view. The Bishop was convinced that to see God as 'up there' or 'out there' in some distant part of the Universe was one of these myths perpetuated through the ages. If we see through the myths, we can find a new meaning relevant to our modern life. God, Jesus and our worship find their roots in Love. Our worship is then directed towards purifying and correcting our lives in the light of Christ's Love and in Him we find the grace and power to be the reconciled and reconciling community.

Of course many parishioners would not have been influenced by the theological debates taking place at the time. Generally in the 1960s, St. Mary's trod a traditional path, which was well supported and, as we have seen, had picked itself up financially and evangelically through Christian Stewardship. At that time Sunday services took place at 8.0 a.m. Holy Communion, at 10.45 a.m. and 6 p.m. The main morning services varied

20. Church interior in the 1960s.   S.G.

with Choral Communion on the first Sunday, a Family Service on the second, Matins followed by Holy Communion on the third and Matins only on the fourth and fifth Sundays. Choral Evensong was sung each Sunday evening. Sunday School met in the Aireville Terrace School at 10.45 a.m. but the members joined a Family Service on each second

Sunday. Parents with young children were sometimes not welcome at Sunday services if they did what children like to do, commenting loudly on what was happening around them. The Parish Magazine for December 1968 consisted of a printed cover with a black and white photograph of the Tryptych and the Altar on the front. Inside were the times of services, and the list of clergy, officials and church organizations. On the back cover was an Advertisers' directory. Four pages then contained the Vicar's letter, various short reports, the calendar of services and meetings, the flower rota, the sidesmen's rota and extracts from the registers. There were two inserts, the Diocesan Newsletter and *Home Words*, the latter being published in London by the Home Words Printing and Publishing Company which had been a feature of the Parish magazine for over fifty years.

When Keith Dodgson was appointed organist and choirmaster in 1968, he recruited good choirboys from the local school where his wife taught, and a high standard was maintained. The Parish Room was given a really good makeover in 1964, with the old fireplace boarded up and the floor made much better, after treatment by the officer responsible for the care of buildings belonging to the West Riding County Council. He was Ernest Peat, who lived nearby and was also a good bass singer in the choir. The plan to have a new Vestry in the South East corner of the church was however set aside amid difficulties over obtaining a faculty. Some members of the PCC thought that changing the interior of the Church was going to require more negotiations and time than the plan was worth.

There was, during John Beardsmore's incumbency, talk of much closer relationships with the Methodists in the village. This reflected discussions going on nationally. From 1968 all communicant members of other churches could take communion in Anglican churches and from 1969 Anglican buildings could be used by other denominations. The second Vatican Council, which had met and deliberated in the early 1960s, led to a thaw in relations between Roman Catholics and Anglicans and this too was beginning to have some effect locally though perhaps more slowly in Burley than elsewhere as dear old Father Scannell held his flock together in traditional ways at the Church of Saints John Fisher and Thomas More in Bradford Road.

The issue of patronage eventually was resolved for St. Mary's in 1966 when the executors of the Cresswells handed the right of advowson over to the Bishop of Bradford. The PCC was relieved to hear that the Bishop was happy to consider approaches from the Parish before making any decisions as to whom to appoint if a vacancy arose. This was timely because in late 1968, Rev. John Beardsmore announced that he had accepted a living in Bromley, Kent and would leave the parish at Easter 1969. The lure of Yorkshire brought him back to the Diocese, to be Vicar of Buttershaw in 1970, from which living he retired in 1988. Since then he has served in the Diocese as a licensed priest.

The Bishop's secretary wrote to the Secretary of the PCC in January 1969 asking for a statement of the conditions, needs and traditions of the Parish. Further it was stated that the Bishop would consult the Churchwardens and the nominated advisers about the appointment[71].

The Parish's reply to the Bishop's request contained the following:
> _Conditions:_ *New housing development, municipal and private, has made the village a dormitory area attracting substantial numbers of young married people whose business or employment is located in the adjacent towns and cities.*
> *There is a growing Sunday School and well established Mothers' Union and Young Wives' groups. Parish finance is by means of a Christian Stewardship Planned Giving Scheme, now in its seventh year, and the PCC has sufficient funds at its disposal to meet normal needs.*
> _The Needs:_ *the PCC feels that the needs of the Parish would best be served by the appointment of a married man, preferably aged 35 – 40 who has already held a living or served as Senior Assistant Curate.*
> _Traditions:_ *The worship of the Parish has always been conducted in a central churchmanship style and it is considered*

essential that the man appointed not be of extreme views one
way or the other. No vestments are worn and the Holy
Communion is celebrated according to Series 2 rites[72].
There was a short interregnum during which Rev. Colston Sage, a retired
priest living in the village, officiated at services.

The **Rev. Donald Bottomley Aldred** was instituted and inducted on 3rd
October 1969. He fitted the requirements of the Parish being 38 years old,
married to Janet with a family of three, Christopher, Susan and Jane, and
having served as Vicar of Gomersal in West Yorkshire. He had qualified at
the University of London as an Associate of King's College in 1955, became a curate at Cudworth and was priested in 1956. His second curacy
was in Heckmondwike from 1959 to 1962 when he moved to be Vicar of
Gomersal.

Donald's arrival in Burley coincided with the 50th anniversary celebrations
of the founding of the Bradford Diocese in 1919. One of the key features
of the Jubilee Year was an exercise for Parishes called the Consideration,
which was initiated by Bishop Parker. The life and work of each parish
was to be considered by both clergy and laity in relation to
The Church's ministry to adults, young people and children,
The life of the local community,
The worldwide mission of the Church[73].
The parochial reports were presented at the end of the Jubilee year on 29th
June 1970 in front of packed gatherings at St. George's Hall and the
Cathedral in Bradford in the presence of the Archbishop of Canterbury,
Michael Ramsey.

In Burley the new Vicar had worked hard to organise group meetings
which would involve as many parishioners as possible from December
1969 to March 1970. Groups numbering from 6 to 30 members met for
eight one hour sessions mainly in the Parish Room. Over a hundred people
altogether attended the meetings. At these morning, afternoon or evening
sessions, chaired mainly by the Vicar, discussion sheets based on the
Bishop's programme were used. From these the Burley report was

compiled, obviously giving Donald valuable information about the changes people felt necessary to meet the demands of the late twentieth century. It ran to nearly 5000 words and covered issues such as buildings, administration, pastoral work, lay participation in religious services, ecumenical relations and mission. Some of these points had been raised in earlier years such as those suggested by Churchwarden Eric Maufe in the first report on Christian Stewardship (see above).

> *One thing that all members of the discussion groups had in common was a deep concern for the future of our church and for the meaning of our Christian faith….[Emphasis was put on] a desire to hold on to what is seen as good in well practised, traditional forms of worship and missionary enterprise; a wish to make some changes which could improve the Church, such as in the buildings or in the timing of our worship, or in the approach to particular sections of the membership and other outside bodies; a hope for far reaching changes resulting from the implications of the 'new theology' which is seen to relate to widely expressed desires for greater participation in the church and involvement in community action…Perhaps the most important thing that our strategy for the future should contain is the notion that more of our membership should be involved[74].*

What we can see here is the expression of a congregation that had now changed completely since the time of Charles Ingham Black's incumbency. The desire to be involved in and be active not passive recipients of teaching and pastoral care, had grown during the twentieth century. There were more people in the parish able and willing to take on and share in the leading roles and it was clearly Donald Aldred's task to continue the revolution. A new chapter in the religious life of Burley was being written.

CHAPTER SIX

BUILDING FOR THE FUTURE, 1970 TO 2000

*The social order in which nominal church membership was an
accepted fact has gone for good and it is no use bemoaning the
fact...The fact that increased material prosperity and security
have been accompanied by a sharp decline in the outward
practice of religion only suggests how nominal much of this
former adherence was in the earlier times*[75].

Rev Donald Aldred had other matters beside the Consideration to deal with
in his first years as Vicar of Burley. Our summary of it above perhaps
needs to be tempered by the Bishop of Bradford's thoughts, as indicated by
the short quotation at the beginning of this chapter. When we remember
that the electoral roll stood at over 900 in the 1920s and in 1969/70 it was
only 299, some indication is given of the change in nominal allegiance to

21. Rev. Donald Aldred AKC and his wife Janet.

the Church and the work that would have to be done if some of the hopes expressed in the Consideration were to be realised.

As ever, there were a number of ongoing maintenance problems which needed urgent attention. The minutes of the Vicar's first PCC note that considerable expenditure was required on the vicarage and the Church. The organ needed attention and the decoration of the nave and chancel required refreshing. Keith Dodgson, the organist appointed in 1968 spent much time in persuading the PCC to undertake a major overhaul of the organ. At his first Annual Vestry and Parochial meeting, the vicar congratulated Keith for 'his wonders with music' considering the state of the organ. [It was not until 1971 that work commenced on it.] At that meeting Jim Slater and Sam Wheeler were elected as churchwardens and Jim Bennett was the PCC secretary. For the first time elections to the new Deanery Synod were made and the representatives were to be Jim Bennett, Nigel Cottam and John Rayner.

Synodical government of the Church of England had received Royal assent in 1969. From then on an assembly of three houses, Bishops, Clergy and Laity, was to adjudicate on and recommend changes in the work and mission of the Church of England. There were also Diocesan and Deanery Synods, made up from clergy and laity. The new Deanery Synod was formed around the Parish of Otley, on similar lines to the previous ruridecanal conferences. The Deanery Synod was possibly the weakest link in the system for it could only debate and vote on resolutions to send to the Diocesan Synod, or provide discussion and training for laity concerning parochial issues[76]. It had no financial resources and it provided for participation without power, sitting uneasily between parish and diocese. However, Deanery Synod members could be elected to the Diocesan Synod, and some of St. Mary's representatives were elected to serve on the higher body, where they had a greater voice. In 1973, Nigel Cottam and the Vicar were voted on to the Diocesan body. Nigel also was elected on to the influential Bishop's advisory committee. The Diocese was and is of course represented on the General Synod.

One of the major achievements of the new Vicar was the completion of long desired alterations to the church building to accommodate the choir, children's work and social gatherings. Plans for a church extension were revived in the Parish Consideration and in 1974, at a meeting of the PCC, the Vicar requested firm action commenting that for five years at least there had been nothing much beyond discussion. A committee was then formed to draw up a brief for an architect which would provide the facilities needed. The first idea that they came up with was for a separate building on the north side of the Church. In September 1975 the architects appointed were in favour of a stone-built extension on the south side adjacent to the Vicar's vestry, along with a balcony in the nave at the west end to provide more accommodation. Approaches were made to the Diocese and general approval was given to the idea of an extension on the south side of the church. The balcony idea was later dropped. In early 1976 there was a further complication because a committee of representatives of St. Mary's, the Methodist Church and Salem had been discussing whether there should be some sharing of church premises. The first proposal was that St. Mary's should be used for worship by all the congregations and other premises could be kept for mutual benefit as required. When the Methodists indicated that they could not go along with a shared premises scheme, the PCC went ahead and proceeded with the plans for an extension.

An Appeal Committee was set up to raise funds for an extension initially costing £19,000, with Brian Ludlam as its Chairman. Tenders were submitted in May 1977 and by November the appeal had raised £12000. Construction began in the summer of 1977 and was completed in late 1978. In November the new extension was opened with a service of dedication. The final cost was about £4000 over budget, as there had been some complications in connecting the new building to the main drainage system.

Although the idea of sharing premises with other churches in Burley had not come to fruition, there was a growing sense of common interest as all were feeling the effect which the Bishop of Bradford had noted. Numbers in the congregations were falling and young people were not committing themselves as much as in the past. Ever since the Second World War there had been a British Council of Churches and in 1971 Donald Aldred suggested that a local Council of Churches covering Burley and Menston should be formed. Already in January 1970 the Methodist minister in Burley, Bill Tait, had been invited to preach at one of the services of Evensong. Cooperation among the Burley churches began to flourish and in 1975 a Burley Christian Council was formed. The participating churches were the Parish Church, the Methodist Church, Salem United Reformed Church and the Roman Catholic Church of SS John Fisher and Thomas More. The objects were a) to draw the churches into greater understanding and unity, b) to enable the churches to bear a more united witness in the community and to serve it more effectively, c) to give expression to the churches' common faith and devotion, by encouraging united acts of worship and fellowship. One of the community outcomes of this cooperation was the annual summer fete held in Langford Lane for several years at what was then the Burley Middle School[77]. United services were held from time to time usually on a Sunday evening. Joint Lenten observance too became an annual event, with evening lectures and a walk of witness on Good Fridays.

A further joint activity arose out of the growing awareness of the need for aid to developing countries. A Burley Christian Aid Committee had been formed in 1972 with two representatives from each of the four churches. Christian Aid as an organisation grew out of a body called Christian Reconstruction in Europe after the Second World War and was a department of the British Council of Churches. During the 1950s it responded to the needs of Africa and Asia and wanted to 'combat poverty' across the world. The first Christian Aid week in England was held in 1957 and the organisation from the 1960s called itself Christian Aid. The little red envelopes have been dropping through letter boxes annually since then. In Burley we started a little later, therefore, but it has become an annual event with numerous supporters from all the churches. David Unsworth and Margaret Warwick were the first representatives of the PCC to be elected to serve on the committee. As well as support for Christian Aid, missionary giving and grants to other charities by the PCC in 1973 totalled £608 out of total expenditure of £5657.

Relations between the Methodist Church and St. Mary's grew during Donald Aldred's incumbency especially after Rev. Neil Dixon was appointed to be the Methodist Minister in 1975. A lovely true story of their cooperation comes from the time that new residents were getting settled in the large Sandholme private estate. Neil and Donald joined together in a planned visit to every household. Neil would always knock on the door and speak first. "Welcome to Burley. I am the Methodist Minister and invite you to come to my Church on Sunday. If the resident then replied "Oh no, I belong to the Church of England", then Donald would step forward and say, "Yes, I am the Vicar, please come to my Church on Sunday". They left visiting cards if there was no-one at home. This was paralleled of course by Father Scannell, the Roman Catholic Priest, who visited too, and if he got no response would leave a Nuttall's Minto on the doorstep[78].

Visiting the Parish was also organised in a more systematic way during Donald's time. In 1973 he asked for volunteers to deliver Parish Magazines to all parts of Burley and they were required in addition to keep an eye on people in the streets they visited. Annie Garrett was the first secretary of the Church Area Representatives. She noted in her report to the Annual Parochial Church Meeting in February 1974 that the year began with 48 visitors and increased to 50. They delivered 600 magazines bi-monthly and also birthday cards to the under 5s who had been baptised at St. Mary's. After Annie Garrett, Betty Bentley was responsible for organizing the representatives. They met with the Vicar regularly to report on and discuss any problems. Donald also introduced weekly Church news sheets, which were compiled and duplicated on Saturday nights in the Vicarage.

There were several organisations at the time, which seemed to take on a new lease of life. During the early years of Donald's time in Burley, the

Sunday School continued to attract large numbers of village children. Audrey Birch was in charge of the Sunday School or Junior Church as it was called. Audrey had started teaching as a teenager in 1942 (and continued to do so for over 50 years). Gail Boole became involved with it at the end of the 1960s and she it was who organised a grand summer outing to Scarborough, when 240 children, parents and helpers went by special train. Reports written for the Parochial Church Annual Meetings in the 1970s reveal the numbers of children meeting in the Aireville Terrace School and in the Parish Room at that time. An average of over ninety of the over fives attended the main department with around twenty under fives meeting in the Parish Room with Gail Boole. The number of teachers and helpers varied but for instance in 1975 with ninety six children on roll Audrey Birch had seven staff and four helpers in the School. The children officially attended Church once a month and on special occasions like Mothering Sunday. Gail and her assistants continued in the Parish Room for four years after the main Sunday School had transferred to the Church Lounge in 1983. There were misgivings about the change of venue. Sunday School had for years provided a Church presence in the western part of the village. As elsewhere in the country Sunday School attendance was declining, but the new Church Lounge could not easily cater for the thirty children who attended in the 1980s even with the use of the old choir vestry for some of the older ones. The misgivings about the venue were offset by the desire to encourage parents and children to worship together for at least part of the service in Church.

During the week, a group of 7 – 15 year olds, known as the Adventurers led by Audrey Birch met in the Parish Room on Wednesday evenings and there were 101 on roll in 1973. The aim of the Adventurers 'was to learn about and to help Mission Stations in all parts of the world'[79]. There was a group for the recently confirmed young church members call the Young Christians' Association, meeting fortnightly with Glynne Edwards, who was the new Headteacher of the Aireville Terrace School, and Bill Pickles, a bank manager, and later Ivan Maxted, a college lecturer, as leaders. A Bible Study Group met regularly with Raymond Gill, at that time a Lay Reader.

The Mothers' Union led by Mrs Gill Kilner had 67 members in the mid-seventies of whom 25 – 30 attended meetings regularly. Members had become involved with the new Burley Good Neighbours scheme, the Luncheon Club, with serving tea to the Old People's Welfare and raising funds for Overseas Groups of the Mothers' Union. Younger women church members met as the Young Wives, and they had 32 members with an average attendance of 21. Their programme included talks by visiting speakers like Mr. Naylor of the Wharfedale Children's Hospital, visits to such places as Hawksworth Hall School, a Special Needs School, and outings in the summer months. There was an annual social when the Mothers' Union and Young Wives met together. They also helped with events like the Supper Club, organised by the Social Activities Committee under the Chairmanship of Nigel Cottam. Some will also remember the planned visit to the York Mystery Plays, which were unfortunately cancelled in 1973, due to heavy rain.

The Vicar in reviewing events in 1977 at the Annual Parochial Church Meeting, noted that he had been helped in his pastoral work by a retired clergyman, Rev Colston Sage, and a non-stipendiary priest, Rev Geoffrey Buckley. They had enabled him to fit in his three half days as Chaplain at Scalebor Park Hospital. He spoke glowingly of all the above mentioned organisations, which meant a much more increased participation in church oriented activities. The appeals for the renewal of the organ and for the extension to the Church had also engendered more support.

A new Church of England Controlled School, Burley and Woodhead First School, had been built on Sandholme Drive, replacing the old school which had closed on the green at Woodhead. There were some discussions about whether it should be a controlled school but they were held in the official Ilkley Education Committee and settled without public dispute. The village schools had been reorganised in 1972 and children aged 9 to 13 were placed in Burley Middle School, a new school eventually built on a site in Langford Lane. The two other schools were renamed First Schools , taking children up to 9 years. Frank Newbould the head of Burley CE First School on Aireville Terrace shared his premises for one year

22. Frank Newbould is seen here receiving retirement gifts from the Vicar and Marie Sutcliffe, the deputy head.   Wharfedale Newspapers

with the new Middle School, but retired at the end of the 1972-73 school year. The headteachers of the three new schools, Glynne Edwards, replacing Frank at Burley CE First School on Aireville Terrace, Ann Bell from Burley and Woodhead CE First School and Leslie Hall from Burley Middle, were coopted on to the PCC. Glynne became secretary to the PCC, after Jim Bennett retired in 1976, thus restoring the tradition that a village Headteacher should occupy the role.

Two years later, in 1979, Donald Aldred gave another optimistic report of activities in the Parish. The extension had been completed and was in use. A Mission to the Parish had been held in Holy Week, with participation of all the Churches in Burley and the presence young theological students had been particularly helpful. Larger congregations were now being recorded. The Parish Communion was attracting about 130 communicants per week and Christian Giving yielded an extra £1000 in 1976. The Electoral Roll had risen to 503 in 1976 and to 552 in 1979. Giving to Missions and other Charities amounted to £1393 out of an expenditure of £18,311. The Vicar noted, however, that there were three distinct congregations on Sundays, at

8 o'clock Communion, the Parish Communion later in the morning and at Evensong. The second was attended by the majority of parishioners, but Evensong was still popular. The Parish was fortunate to have the help of two other ordained ministers and two lay readers.

The decade had begun with an appeal so that the organ could renovated. Nigel Cottam chaired the Hundred Day Appeal Fund to raise £1000. The target was reached as a result of numerous efforts and it was supplemented by transfers from the Church accounts. About £2000 was spent on the instrument, so facilitating a wider range of music. Keith Dodgson, organist at the time, in his report to the Annual Parochial Meeting in February 1971, said that there were 20 boys in the choir and a waiting list, as well as 10 men. The numbers were restricted because of the small size of the Vestry. Michael Hodges, a sixth form pupil at Ilkley Grammar School, replaced Keith when the latter went to live in Scotland in January 1971. Michael had already been an assistant organist and choir master at Worth Parish Church in Sussex. The family moved to Ilkley when Michael's father was appointed Treasurer to Ilkley Urban District Council. Michael's inspired leadership led the choir to achieve a consistently high standard. He was fortunate in having two young singers, Andrew Arundel and Vernon Young, who had outstanding musical ability and could lead the others. Most choirboys too remained members until their voices broke, gaining confidence and skills to match the best in the English Choral Tradition. A recording is still available of Mendelssohn's *Hear My Prayer*, which illustrates this.

Not only did the choir sing at regular Sunday services, but with the Vicar's prompting a tradition of Advent Carol Services on the First Sunday in Advent began. These services attracted large congregations with standing room only for some. In 1976, when Michael had returned from taking his music degree at Durham University, the Advent service was reviewed by the music critic of the *Yorkshire Post*, Ernest Bradbury:

> *All the choral music was very well sung, not least the contribu-*
> *tions from the boy choristers who, drilled into a fine awareness*
> *of the use of consonants and able to produce an agreeably*

smooth tone, took the lead with confidence and conviction. The
adult section of the choir was augmented by a number of other
choristers from the area[80].
The boys also for the first time during these years sang at the Midnight
Mass on Christmas Eve, which was one of the highlights of their year,
especially as it was preceded by carol singing at some of the houses in

23. **Choir boys, 1973**. L.toR. Back row: D. Warwick, V. Young, I. Wilkie,
C. Wardle;   Middle row: A. Arundel, N. Walters, P. Warwick, B. Thompson,
C. Aldred, I. McGowan, R. Ogden;   Front row: J. Breare, F. Young ; K. Clayton;
D. Thompson, C. Ogden, P. Ogden.   Photo by M. Hodges

24. Michael Hodges organist

Burley and at Scalebor Hospital.
After refreshments in the home of one
of the senior boys who lived close to
the Church, they miraculously
recovered their composure in time for
the service.

The good choral tradition continued
during the 1970s even though the

organists changed. After Michael went to Durham in the autumn of 1973, his place was taken by Keith Newell and he was followed by Malcolm Spencer. Keith was for instance the organist at a Service of Ten Favourite Hymns, chosen in a ballot by the congregation, on 21st September 1975[81]. Since then similar services have been held from time to time. When Malcolm left in 1976, Michael returned for a short spell while working in a bank in Ilkley. Thereafter Joan Ravens (later Mrs Lewis Ogden) took on this role. She had been organist and director of music in a number of Leeds churches, and was the first woman to be organist at St. Mary's. Both her sons sang with the choir and the younger of the two, Simon, has made a career in Early Music.

During these years on Saturday afternoons an additional activity for the choir boys and some of their parents was the Choir Football Team. The Vicar, a keen football supporter, named them the Burley Angels. His son Christopher was part of the team and his wife Janet was a regular part of the touchline crowd. They played in a white strip and competed in the Bradford Diocesan Choir League. At first when they were the new boys on the block they were heavily defeated, but after two seasons they became the Champions. Their team song was a parody on the carol *Angels from the Realms of Glory* written by the Vicar. Some of the outstanding singers were the best footballers.

Church music was and is a very important part of the worship of the congregation. During the 1970s there was a change taking place in the pattern of worship. The limited introduction of a new eucharist in the 1960s marked the beginning of an era when the Parish Communion became the centre of Sunday worship. Donald Aldred embraced this change. Alternative forms of Holy Communion to that in the Book of Common Prayer were published by a Liturgical Commission from the 1960s and these were known as Series 1, 2 and 3 versions. John Beardsmore had accepted the use of Series 2 once a month and the congregation commented favourably on the whole for this move away from the older version. With the new incumbent, the final revision to Series 3 became the main service for Sunday morning worship. The key

25. The Burley Angels 1973. Left to right: Back row: V. Young, I. Wilkie, A. Arundel, D. Warwick; Middle row: N. Walters, K. Clayton, J. McGowan, F. Young, J. Breare, P. Warwick; Front row: D. Thompson, B. Thompson. [Missing: C. Aldred.]
Photo: M. Hodges

aspect of all the revisions was in the participation of the laity in the readings, the intercessions, and the presentation of the elements at the offertory. The celebrant marked this change by facing westward towards the congregation. Lay readers, such as John Rayner, Raymond Gill and Jonathan Atkinson were regularly involved in the administration of the chalice to communicants. Then permission was granted by the Bishop to other members of the congregation to assist the celebrant in this way, a practice that continues to this day. Approval by the PCC and the Bishop is necessary for the laity to be involved in administering the chalice. Among the first members of the congregation to be so licensed were Frank Newbould and Kelvin Newberry. Later Frank Schofield and Janet Aldred, the Vicar's wife, also joined them.

To some worshippers the changes in the wording and the practice of the Eucharist meant a loss of familiar patterns and caused some misgivings. For those who had been brought up with the traditional prayers for the Church Militant, and the 1662 versions of the Confession and the Prayer of Humble Access, the changes could seem a step too far. Only after years of the use of the new service with its less formal language were the traditionalists reconciled. Four alternative Eucharistic Prayers caused some eyebrows to be raised, but here and in the country as a whole, the 'process had been remarkable for the absence of doctrinal bitterness and controversy which was in sharp contrast to the sad discord which had accompanied the Prayer Book Revision in the years leading up to 1927'[82]. As in many other Anglican churches, the PCC decided to keep the use of the Book of Common Prayer version for the 8 o'clock Communion service. In 1980 the process of liturgical revision was sealed by the publication in one volume of the new services under the title of the Alternative Service Book. St. Mary's purchased 250 of these in 1981. There was some consternation about the size of the volumes but this was alleviated by the introduction of coloured ribbons to mark key parts of the services.

The times of services changed towards the end of Donald Aldred's ministry. As the Parish Communion had become the main service of Sunday worship, and numbers of communicants increased, there was a sense of congestion at some celebrations. A Family Service had been introduced at this time and quite soon there was a request that this service should be a Eucharist. In the autumn of 1981 the idea was adopted once a month at 9.20 a.m., and the music led by a small orchestra directed by Yvonne Edwards. It was not long before there were requests for this service to become a weekly event.

Along with the move towards a more sacramental form of worship there was a desire to provide an aumbry where the sacrament could be reserved for later use. Though this went against the traditions of the Parish, as outlined to the Bishop in 1969 before Donald's appointment, there was enough support for one to be provided. There had been a request for an aumbry in 1974 but a decision was deferred. Finally, it was put in place on the wall to the left of the altar, at the expense of the Garrett family in memory of Annie, in 1978. Vestments for use in the Eucharist were also obtained and, in 1980, Ian Walsh made a special chest for storing them in the Vicar's vestry.

Donald Aldred announced in the summer of 1983 that he would be leaving the Parish to take up the living of Holy Trinity Parish Church, Skipton. He was leaving what was on the whole a thriving parish in which he and his wife were much loved. They had brought joy to many people in their work together, and moved the worship and activities of the church forward.

During his ministry, Donald Aldred was supported by a number of other ordained priests. Colston Sage and Geoffrey Buckley have already been mentioned. Two other retired Priests came to live in Burley, either to be near family or simply to find a pleasant place in which to retire. Canon Tom Levesley, formerly Vicar of St. Margaret's in Ilkley, came to the village to be nearer his daughter and son-in-law, Susan and Peter Settle. Rev. Eric T. Bosley, who had been ordained later in life, had served in Africa and retired in 1975. He went first to Keighley and then came to live in Iron Row in 1980. Though quite elderly by that time, he was able to give some support for a few years. With permission to serve in the Diocese, all were helpful in allowing the Vicar to spread out his work and to take well earned rests. Several Lay Readers served the parish. John Rayner, Raymond Gill and Jonathan Atkinson are mentioned above, but in 1979 our very first woman Lay Reader took up her duties. She was Lois Fulker, who had trained while being a very active member of the congregation[83]. 1979 was the first year in which women were allowed to enter the Order of Lay Readers. The Deanery Synod began to consider the issue of allowing women to be ordained into the Church's ministry, but at this time in the 1980s there was much doubt and opposition.

The vital role of churchwarden was filled by some long serving men during the 1970s and early 1980s. Jim Slater retired from his role as Vicar's warden in 1973 after holding the post for 27 years. Sam Wheeler retired after six years as People's warden in 1972 and in his place Pip Hayes was elected. From 1973, the distinction between Vicar's and People's warden was dropped and the churchwardens were simply elected as wardens. Jim Slater had also been the Treasurer for the Church's accounts and Pip Hayes inherited that role.

Harry Hornby served from 1973 until 1981 when Rex Madin was elected. Pip and Rex were the wardens who had to administer the parish during the interregnum, between the departure of Donald Aldred and the arrival of the next incumbent.

The PCC held regular monthly meetings during this time. Some members served on the PCC for most the 1970s and early 1980s. These included Nigel Cottam, the secretary, Glynne Edwards, Raymond Gill, John Rayner (who died in 1980), Mabel Baxter, Audrey Birch, and Sue Settle. Members were elected initially for three years and could stand again for a further term. By becoming an

26. Churchwarden Jim Slater retired in 1973, after 27 years, and was presented with a gold watch.
Wharfedale Newspapers

ex-officio member, such as a Diocesan or Deanery Synod member or Lay Reader, some could stay on the PCC longer. That was obviously a useful device because members with long experience could give advice at times of change or disagreement. There were some questions raised in Annual Meetings about the longevity of membership, but generally sound wisdom prevailed.

Routine business to do with accounts, church buildings and their maintenance, church organisations and mission were the important items on the PCC agenda. Incidentally much of the necessary secretarial support for the PCC and the Church generally was provided by Janet Aldred and Jay Hayes. The amount of the Parish Share, or Diocesan Quota, as it was sometimes called, was a frequently occurring item, since it took up an increasing proportion of the Church budget. During Donald Aldred's ministry, several special issues caused debates where disagreement had to be minuted. The Church's attitude to nuclear weapons, the admission of women to the priesthood, the form which religious education should take in schools, the role the parish should play in youth work, and the part that church music and the choir should play in services were all controversial subjects.

There was a special meeting of the PCC about Church music in May 1982, when a proposal to have a mixed choir was debated. Some disquiet about the choir had been voiced in the previous year. Women and girls had sung in the choir occasionally, and it was said that it was unfair to expect them to be there on special occasions only. However after discussion, Frank Newbould put a resolution that 'for the present we remain a male choir', which was carried by 7 votes for, 6 against and 3 abstentions.

The situation of the Church on one side of a busy main road through the village and the difficulty of crossing it safely were constantly being raised. When the Highways Authorities decided in 1983 that a by-pass should be built on a line to the north of Main Street and one plan was for it to run between the church and the vicarage, there was much alarm. A public enquiry followed and the issue was shelved for another decade.

A lively account of the activities of the senior Young Christian Association (14 – 18 age group) had been given in the report to the Annual Parochial Church meeting of 1980 by Janet Aldred, the leader. The membership was about 20 and the group met fortnightly on Sunday evenings and once a month on Fridays in the Parish Room. The emphasis was on Faith, Fun and Fellowship. Sunday evening meetings included talks, games and quizzes, ending with the office of compline, which 'has a calming influence on us all'. Janet's belief was that 'the Church needs to attract young people in

110

order to win, build and send them out into the world by appealing to their physical, social and spiritual needs'.

The Parish Magazine had its ups and downs. Its production was often a collaborative effort and much depended upon a succession of people to fill the various roles. In 1973 a new style magazine had been favourably received, according to the PCC minutes, and it was reaching a third of the households in the village. A new contract with printers called the Delta Press had been arranged from the end of 1974, and John Gott was to be the compiler with the Vicar as general editor. Production continued smoothly for a time until the Gotts left the village in 1980. No-one came forward to be the compiler and the Vicar felt that he could not take on the whole job. For over a year there was no magazine. A new bulletin began to be produced in the summer of 1982 and finally at the end of the year, production of a monthly magazine began again with Joan Roper as editor. She continued to do this until 1987.

The last year of Donald Aldred's ministry coincided with the 140th anniversary of the foundation of St. Mary's, and he wanted this to be celebrated. Discussions about the form of the celebration continued for several months. It was finally organised by Janet Aldred. A day of celebration was held on the Vicarage Lawn on 12th June 1983 which included a communion service followed by a picnic. In church there was an exhibition of documents and photographs illustrating 140 years of church life. On the Sunday nearest the actual anniversary, 19th June, the Archdeacon of Craven preached at a special Parish Communion. The following Sunday, children from the Sunday School did a dramatic re-enactment of the rites of consecration of 1843.

Donald Aldred's last attendance at a PCC meeting was on 6th December 1983. At that meeting the Archdeacon of Bradford, Rev Frank Sargeant, was present in order to engage the Council in a discussion of the previous ten years and thoughts about the future. He was about to leave the Diocese and so thoughts were very much on the changing situation. The minutes of the PCC record that concerns were expressed about the decline in the number of men coming forward for the ministry. At the same time there was optimism about the number of women who were offering themselves for theological training. Lay involvement was seen to be increasing and the notion of "shared ministry" was being promulgated.

After three church services on 8th January 1984, a reception was held in the Queen's Hall in Burley, when the congregation was invited to say farewell to Donald and Janet, and their family. About six hundred attended and enjoyed a buffet lunch. The churchwardens, Rex Madin and Pip Hayes, made presentations, which included a cloak for Donald, a china owl for Janet (a favourite mascot) and a cheque for £1500, along with an album with a thousand signatures[84]. Donald himself left a gift for the Church, a ciborium, which was later suitably engraved.

27. Farewell to the Aldreds. Wharfedale Newspapers
L.to R. Susan Aldred, Pip Hayes, Janet Aldred,
Donald Aldred, Jane Aldred, Rex Madin.

With a much increased electoral roll, large congregations for the Parish Communion, and good relations with neighbouring churches, Donald Aldred was able to pass on a well ordered parish to his successor. There was an interregnum of 6 months, but the Churchwardens could call on the services of four retired clergy living in the village. Canon Tom Levesley, Canon Denis Rutt, Rev Colston Sage and Rev Eric Bosley shared the duties, with the first taking the lead. Denis Rutt had retired to Burley in 1983. He served as a priest in South Africa for six years in the 1940s, followed by incumbencies in East Anglia, and then as Canon Residentiary and Precentor of Lichfield Cathedral. During the interregnum in March, the death of Jim Slater was recorded.

At the Annual Parish Meeting in March 1984, it was announced that the **Rev John Tidy, AKC**, would become the new vicar. Born in 1948, he studied at King's College London and S. Augustine's College, Canterbury, being made a deacon in 1973 and priest in 1974. He served in the Durham Diocese and was Vicar of Auckland from 1978 to 1984. He was married to Pamela and had two young daughters Charlotte and Alexa. A third daughter Faith was born in Burley.

Thriving though the Parish might be, it was clear that the Diocese of Bradford was troubled by economic change. The textile industries which had provided employment in the city and inner suburbs for over a century were in decline, and the housing estates which had optimistically been built in the 1930s, 1950s and 1960s to house the working class were showing signs of decay. In the rural areas, too, changes in agriculture were resulting in population decline. The middle class areas in Wharfedale and Airedale were increasingly being called upon to support the Diocese. In parishes like Burley, there were year on year increases in the Parish Share, the sum which the Diocese requires of them to support the stipends of all its clergy and administration.

The problems were graphically brought home by the work of a commission set up in July 1983 by Archbishop Runcie 'to examine the strengths, insights, problems and needs of the Church's life and mission in the Urban Priority Areas and, as a result, to reflect on the challenge which God may be making to Church and Nation: and to make recommendations to appropriate bodies'[85]. Its conclusions showed the stark differences in employment opportunities, rates of illness and death, educational achievement, family breakdown and homelessness, between the poorer areas of town and country, and the wealthier suburban and commuter areas. The Report recommended that there should be cooperation between richer and poorer parishes within Dioceses, and a more equitable distribution of resources amongst the Dioceses. Parish Shares should be justified in terms of the comparative wealth and viability of parishes. At the same time those older Dioceses in more affluent parts of the country should support those not so well off in historical resources.

Following the publication of *Faith in the City* the Archbishop of Canterbury launched the Church Urban Fund in 1988. Each Diocese was given a target for fund raising. Bradford's was a relatively modest sum of £200,000, but even so the outcome of the appeal was disappointing at first, though eventually the sum was raised. An office was set up at 43, Lawn Avenue, Burley to house an appeals' centre for this part of the Diocese. It had previously been used as the residence for Rev Peter Endall, who was the curate at St. Mary's from 1985 to 1988. Later it became for a time an office used by our first woman curate, Rev. Eileen McLean, who came after her ordination as deacon in June 1988.

With increasing amounts to be raised as our Parish Share, the years of John Tidy's ministry were dominated to an extent by financial concerns. In the annual meetings following his arrival, there were repeated discussions about the increases and in 1985, 1986 and 1987 the Share was not paid in full. There had been Christian Stewardship renewal schemes, such as that culminating on Pledge Sunday, 2nd March 1986, and they had enjoyed some limited success, but it was felt that a bigger effort was required. The Diocesan Stewardship Adviser, Rev. Peter Burwell, was invited in 1988 to begin preparations for a campaign in 1989 to raise awareness among members of the congregation of the need to give more. A group of parishioners also went to the Diocesan retreat house at Parceval Hall, near Appletreewick, for a weekend conference. This delightful house has been host to several parish weekends over the years.

Meanwhile a Parish Stock Taking (PST) exercise was carried out in 1987. A map of the village was drawn showing where members of the Electoral Roll lived. A questionnaire was distributed asking respondents about the Church, its services and their commitment to it. The results of this led to discussions in the PCC which formed the basis of a Parish Plan outlining the mission of the Church. From this the PCC recommended the setting up of six sub-groups to monitor communications, resources, pastoral care, worship, outreach and growing in faith. The remit of each group was to make recommendations to the PCC, and in essence this was the origin of the groups which continue into the new millennium. Many ideas flowed

28. On retreat at Parceval Hall, Summer 1988. Members of the congregation with Rev. Eileen McLean, first on left at the front, and Rev John Tidy, last on the right back row.   Photo by D.Sowman

from these deliberations. One notable outcome was the link made between Burley and the Urban Priority Parish of Shelf and Buttershaw. This particularly involved cooperation between St. Mary's and the Church Army officer, Roy Wheatley, on the Buttershaw estate. Fundraising and also appeals for domestic items of equipment were organised by Gail Boole, who regularly visited the estate and worked with the Church Army officer into the 1990s. The link with the Parish of Shelf has continued up to the present. In May 2009 the Mothers' Union was invited to join with the branch there for worship and a consideration of the continuing link. The work of the PST was also carried forward into the Stewardship Mission which was given the overall title of *Forward Together in Faith*. Eileen McLean, the curate, had overall responsibility for preparing the study material, briefing group leaders and allocating members to twelve house groups. Ninety five people were involved in these discussions. Ideas from these meetings were summarised by Eileen McLean and presented to a conference of the congregation on 14th March 1989. Emphasis was placed on encouraging more involvement in the mission of the church and to that end further work was done in the Sunday School and young people's groups. On Sunday 7th May, a Parish Gathering, entitled "Presenting the Challenge", took place at Aireville Terrace School, beginning with a Eucharist, followed by lunch, and afternoon meetings where the outcome was summarised under various themes: 'Children in the Way', 'Communication', 'Outreach' and 'Financial Response'. Children gave a dramatic representation of caring for each other. There was also an exhibition of dance and movement in worship. In conclusion all participants were encouraged to complete the 'My Gifts for God' cards.

The following Sunday there was a service of response. Members of the congregation were invited to bring the cards and their financial pledges to be presented as part of the offertory. The Diocesan Stewardship Adviser preached at this service. In his report to the Parish dated 28th June 1989, he

29. Parish Stock Taking at Aireville Terrace School,

writes:

*Forward together in Faith has been a major exercise in the life
of the congregation of St. Mary's. It has required a great deal
of hard work on the part of the Mission Officers, under the
chairmanship of John Masters. It has been well organised and
incorporated some very imaginative and innovative features.
The whole initiative has been good, especially the involvement
of the young people. The study material was excellent. The
groups were well attended and much enjoyed, and the
Gathering was an undoubted success.*

*Despite this the response from the congregation as a whole has
been very disappointing. To have a less than 30% response in
both offers of gifts and financial pledges is significantly below
the response in other parishes in the Diocese. A congregation
with the mass of talent evident at Burley and the comparative
affluence of its members, still has a lot of its number prepared to
be relatively uninvolved and uncommitted...The level of
financial giving is generally unrealistic and nowhere near the
5% recommended by the General Synod some years ago...A
stewardship mission gives the opportunity to take stock and
become more aware of the current situation...Follow up and
promotion must be vigorously undertaken*[86].

The report was received with expressions of concern, but the PCC agreed
that there must be some follow-up. The parish treasurer, Pip Hayes, felt
that it was necessary to educate people to take on board the thought that
our financial giving is a reflection of our Christian commitment. A
Mission Continuation Group was set up to monitor the implementation of
the Parish Plan and to report back to the Diocesan Stewardship Adviser in
a year's time. One of the decisions was to hold a Gift Day in November.
The urgency of the appeal was stressed by pointing out that currently the
cost of meeting all the church's commitments was about £1000 per week,
but that only £600 was being received. A parish list was drawn up
including all the members on the electoral roll and others who attended
church from time to time. Letters were sent to all of these in late October

with an invitation to a Vigil of Prayer on Friday, 10th November and to the Gift Day on Saturday, 11th November. It was hoped to raise £9000, but the result was disappointing. In the end of year accounts it was stated that £3910 had been received, though promises for more had been made. The Diocesan Share of £36,577 was met that year but only through drawing on the reserves. It is good to note, however, that in 1990 the church's grants to Missions and other charities amounted £11,701 out of a total expenditure of £62,532, compared with £9601 out of a total expenditure £61,095 in 1989.

An appeal was made to the Diocese soon afterwards for a re-examination of the Share allocation, on the grounds that average numbers in the congregation had declined over the previous five years. The appeal was allowed but the reduction agreed was quite small. The Share for 1990 was £35,810 and it was met in full. The Accounts for 1990 show that the Stewardship Mission had had an effect, for income from covenanted giving rose from £20,757 to £25,116 and tax recovered increased by £1400. Other stewardship giving also increased by over £2000. When Rev John Tidy left St. Mary's to become Dean of St. George's Cathedral in Jerusalem at the beginning of 1993, there had been no more defaults on the Diocesan Share.

John was not the only priest in the parish in the 80s. The retired clergy who had assisted during the interregnum continued to help but age took its toll. Denis Rutt was the only one to survive throughout John's incumbency and he celebrated his 50 years as a priest in 1992. Tom Levesley died in 1987. Other somewhat younger clergy came on the scene. Rev. Peter Endall and his wife Christine came to Burley in 1985. Peter was a mature entrant to theological training being ordained deacon in 1985 from Lincoln Theological College. He served as curate for three years, living in the Diocesan property at 43

30. Rev Peter Endall.
Photo: B. Schofield

Lawn Avenue. Youth work was a particular focus of his ministry and he set up the Ichthus[87] Fellowship for the 13+ age group. When he left Burley in 1988, he was appointed Vicar of Thwaites Brow, Keighley

The appointment of the Rev Eileen McLean as curate signified the big change that had occurred in the Anglican Church. She and her husband, Jim, and three sons, were living in Menston when she came in July 1988. There had been debates about admitting women to the priesthood in the Church of England since the 1960s. Other denominations had women ministers from at least that decade. Overseas provinces of the Anglican Communion accepted women from the late 1960s. Women had been accepted as Lay Readers in England from that time too. The General Synod agreed a resolution in 1979 that women ordained overseas could officiate in English churches. The issue remained a very contentious one for the next decade. The PCC here debated the issue in 1983 and by a small majority opposed a resolution approving the ordination of women which was to be put to the Diocesan Synod that summer. However the Diocesan Synod approved the resolution. Indeed the General Synod agreed that women could be ordained deacon in 1988 and eventually following years of acrimonious debate, the measure allowing the full ordination of women as priests was passed in 1992, after Eileen had left Burley.

As we have already noted, Eileen was responsible for organising the Stewardship Mission in Burley. She also led bible study and discussion groups, as well conducting services and carrying out much pastoral visiting. In March 1989, she was interviewed by Jean Endersby for Wharfedale newspapers. Eileen described how she had intended to be a Maths teacher, but that her family commitments, particularly in looking after three growing sons, had not allowed her to enter teaching. Her parents had brought her up as a Roman Catholic, but she entered the Church of England and became very involved in Menston Parish Church. It was there that friends suggested that she should seek ordination. Modestly she said 'it seemed the right sort of idea'. A part time ordination course in Manchester for three years led to her being ordained in 1988. Her interview revealed that she hoped to become a priest though at the time it was impossible and she was not sure that it would ever happen[88]. Of course with hindsight we know it did, for she was made a priest in 1992 and went on to serve in the Diocese of Southwell as a curate. In 1998 she was made Area Dean for parishes in the centre of Nottingham and in 2002 she was appointed Vicar of Bamburgh and Ellingham in the Diocese of Newcastle. Rev Diana (Di) Halliday was appointed curate at St. Mary's after Eileen left in 1992. She too had studied on the part time ordination course being made deacon in 1992 and priest in 1994.

Even with the help of assistant curates, John Tidy did not wish to see the continuation of two Sunday morning services at 9.15 and 10.30. The earlier one had been instituted in Donald Aldred's time to relieve congestion at the Parish Communion and to give scope for a less traditional pattern of worship. John's reasons for its discontinuance were that it was creating two diverse congregations and putting too much pressure on the celebrant to finish promptly. Occasionally there was a queue down the church path waiting for the earlier service to finish. The change from 10.30 to 9.45 for the main service was welcomed by most worshippers. The 8 o'clock said communion provided a quieter service for a small but loyal number of communicants. Evensong continued weekly but as in most parishes was attended by fewer people than in the past, with sometimes as many in the choir as in the congregation. In 1987 too a change was made from *Ancient and Modern Revised* to the *New English Hymnal* for congregational singing.

31. Andrew Dibb, organist
J. Dibb

A series of organists followed Joan Lewis Ogden's resignation in 1982, until the youngest ever organist, Andrew Dibb, was appointed in May 1986. At fourteen he was already a good musician, having played the piano for several years and the organ for a year. He had been a member of the choir and was therefore fully aware of the role of church music at St. Mary's. David Mewis, a

32. Choir Boys of 1983: L.toR. Back row: J. Fryatt, R. Fryatt, A. Dibb, E. Hoyle. Middle row: J. Singleton, M. Stockdale, D. Holbrook, D. Lofthouse, T. Singleton Front row: R. Smith, M. Woodhead, D. Smith.   J. Dibb

member of the congregation at that time, acted as choir master and this arrangement continued until 1990. In that year Andrew went off to Hull University where he had gained an organ scholarship and David Mewis was ordained as deacon in July after a part-time ordination course. During these years the choir maintained a very good standard with some boys gaining awards in Church Music. For instance, Alexander Lilly, the head chorister in 1990, gained the St. Nicholas Award, the highest level of achievement recognised by the Royal School of Church Music, after winning the chorister class in the Wharfedale Music Festival.

Paul Allan was appointed both organist and choirmaster in 1990, a post which he was to hold for eighteen years. He inherited a good choir of around fifteen boys and continued to develop its work and achievements in the 1990s. In 1994 seven of the boys were invited by the Royal School of Church Music to take part in the annual Royal British Legion Festival of Remembrance at the Albert Hall in London. After that service they drove back to Burley to be at the village 10.45 Remembrance Service. Joan

Ogden continued throughout this time as assistant organist. Mrs Betty Carson and her daughter Jennifer gave very valuable support to the choir acting as a kind of matronly influence and looking after choir robes. Together they did this work for many years and since her mother's death, Jennifer has continued it. Rehearsals for the choir were enhanced by the purchase of an electronic piano for the Church Lounge in 1988.

The buildings and fabric of the church were under regular quinquennial scrutiny and in 1984 the bad news was delivered to the PCC that dampness in the south wall of the nave and dry rot in the roof beams would need serious attention. Rewiring and redecoration were also deemed necessary. The spire was in a dangerous condition after storm damage in 1988 and all these items made expenditure essential. Repairs were undertaken and the expense led to the budgetary crises which had occurred earlier in the 1980s. Some of the proceeds of the Gift Day in 1989 had to be used to pay for the repairs, which came to over £30,000. Indeed further appeals had to be made to cover the cost. The Church itself was felt to be inadequate for both congregational services and Sunday School now that the village school was no longer used. Considerations were given to a prefabricated building on the north side, but this idea was soon abandonned because of planning constraints in the Village Conservation Area[89]. Sympathetic developments on the north and western sides of the Church seemed possible, but they would require further appeals for funds. Nothing came of these, but there was a change on the east outside the existing boundary, when a piece of land (known as the piggery) belonging to Burley Hall was purchased to extend the Garden of Rest. Two anonymous donors paid for this in 1987. At the same time a Book of Remembrance for those whose ashes were interred there was placed on the lectern by the pulpit.

Some changes were made in the internal fabric to harmonise with the liturgical changes introduced since the 1970s. The altar was moved westwards to enable the president at the Eucharist to face the congregation. The font was repositioned eastward in 1991, so that all the congregation could participate in baptisms conducted during the parish communion. The space which the font had occupied was given over to a bookstall and a chest from which service sheets and books could be distributed. Robert and Margaret Auty took on the role of maintaining the book stall from this time, which they have continued to do into the new millennium.

Much of the work behind the scenes connected with Church finance, repairs and changes in the building, and the purchase of land, fell to volunteers particularly the churchwardens, the treasurer, the stewardship secretary and other members of the PCC. There were suggestions for the appointment of an administrator, but they were never implemented. The churchwardens at the beginning of John Tidy's ministry were Rex Madin and Pip Hayes. Pip retired to become Church treasurer in 1985, and Ian Walsh began his period as warden which was to last for the rest of John's time. After Rex Madin retired in 1985, Frank Schofield served for four years until he began his training to be a Lay Reader in September 1991. Keith Dale was elected to be churchwarden in his stead. Keith and Ian then managed the interregnum from December 1992, when John Tidy resigned his living to become Dean of St. George's Cathedral, to September 1993. Glynne Edwards was secretary of the PCC until 1987 when he retired and Arthur Woodhead replaced him, having relinquished his role as Electoral Roll officer. Glynne's predecessor Jim Bennett died in 1987. Ben Downs was the stewardship secretary when John Tidy commenced his ministry, and he was succeeded by Frank Schofield who in turn was followed by Bert Taylor. Bert had also been very assiduously looking

33. Rev John Tidy and his wife Pam at St. George's Cathedral, Jerusalem

after the church buildings on behalf of the wardens prior to this. Audrey Birch celebrated her 50th anniversary as a Sunday School teacher in October 1992, a role which she was to carry on into the new millennium. All these and many others were the continuing torch bearers for St. Mary's and, like Audrey, would say 'the church is a way of life'[90].

34. Audrey Birch
Wharfedale Newspapers

On 27th December 1992, in the Aireville Terrace School many members of the congregation enjoyed a buffet lunch at a farewell ceremony and presentation for John Tidy. He made a thank you speech in which he mentioned all those who had played a significant part in his 8½ year ministry in Burley. It was amusingly interrupted by the 'meowing' of an electronic cat, the property since Christmas Day of John's youngest daughter Faith! A day later John and his family set off to fly to Jerusalem, where he took up his new ministry. During March 1993 and again in October 1994, he welcomed pilgrimages from Burley to the Holy Land. The first was organised by Frank Schofield and the second by Bill Pickles. John remained Dean of St. George's until 1997 when he returned to England as Vicar of SS Andrew and Mark, Surbiton, Surrey. He later had another spell in Jerusalem, before migrating to Florida to become Vicar of Miami Beach in 2008. An Icon in the form of a crucifix above the pulpit was John Tidy's gift to the Church.

During the interregnum Canon Denis Rutt and Deacon Di Halliday took the services, assisted occasionally by Rev Lionel Clare from Ilkley. Several former priests also came to officiate, including John Beardsmore, Donald Aldred[91], Graham Betteridge and Eileen McLean. At this time the church celebrated its 150th anniversary. Preparations for it were very intensive and included a major refurbishment of the interior of the Church during May and June. Though this required considerable scaffolding, services continued throughout the time. On 13th June, the Archbishop of

York, the Most Rev John Habgood, preached at the Parish Communion. The main anniversary service was held on 20th June, at which the Right Rev David Smith, Bishop of Bradford, presided and preached. During the weekend of 10th/11th July the church housed an exhibition of the archives and other memorabilia celebrating the church's history, together with a display of children's work from church groups and local schools. An open air service took place on 11th July followed by a picnic on the vicarage lawn. The Bishop of Rochester, the Right Reverend Michael Turnbull, visited the church in August, soon after the announcement that he was to succeed David Jenkins as the Lord Bishop of Durham. Michael Turnbull, brother of James, was born and brought up in Burley.

In the weekend of 10th/11th September, just after Peter's arrival there was a Flower Festival in which many village organisations took part. A History of the Church was compiled and published by Frank Newbould and anniversary beakers and tea towels commemorating the event were put on sale. Frank was also able to celebrate seventy years' association with St. Mary's choir during this time, and was presented with a medal by the Royal School of Church Music. That same month Frank Schofield completed his training and was licensed as a lay reader.

35. Mothers' Union Flower Festival display, 1993.

Rev Peter Sutcliffe came to Burley having been a team vicar in Warwick and a religious affairs producer for BBC Coventry and Warwickshire

Radio. He was a graduate of the College of St. Hild and St. Bede, in the University of Durham, in 1980, and completed his studies at Lincoln Theological College in 1982. He was made Deacon in 1982 and Priest in 1983 and served his first curacy at Christchurch in Skipton, from 1982 to 1985. With his wife Alison and their two children Clare and Tim, Peter settled into the vicarage and quickly began to establish himself in the parish after his installation on 4th September 1993.

36. Rev Peter Sutcliffe   37. Alison Sutcliffe

There were problems for the new Vicar. In particular there was a request from the Diocese to raise almost £1 million pounds from the parishes over six years. The Church Commissioners' resources had been depleted through huge losses on the stock markets in the economic crisis of 1992, and they had reduced their funding to all dioceses including Bradford. The Parish Share for 1993 rose to over £48,000. Inspection of the church roof revealed serious problems and it was estimated that the cost of repairs would reach £30,000. An appeal for the roof was started with Ian Penny acting as organiser. This led to the money being raised by 1995 and the roof repaired. To mark the completion a capsule containing scrapbooks of village life, a newspaper from 1945, a copy of the *Ilkley Gazette* containing an account of the recently completed Burley by-pass on the A65 road, and a copy of *Eminent Victorians, The Forsters of Burley-in-Wharfedale* published in 1994 was hidden in the roof timbers. The roof appeal was so successful that a surplus was achieved and this was put to use to create a ramp for disabled access and to buy a recorder to make tapes of services. A year later the organ also needed extensive repairs estimated to cost £19,000 but this was met by a large donation from Frank Newbould.

This generosity from parishioners was further evidenced when after hearing of the sudden death of former vicar Donald Aldred in 1993, an appeal was made for a memorial seat to be put in the Pudding Tree Garden. The garden had recently been developed by the Burley Community Council in the parcel of land between the Malt Shovel and Cornmill Lane by the entrance to the church. The memorial was also for Donald's wife Janet, who had died of cancer in 1990. The appeal was made by a committee of parishioners whose members were Angela Pickard, Rachel O'Connor, Brenda Chapman, Kath Bennett, Margaret Sumner and Sue Hay. £800 was raised on the first day and so much extra was given that it was possible also to buy a pair of oak acolyte candlesticks to be placed in the church and to give a sum of money towards the upkeep of the Garden. Gifts to missions and other charities also continued at over ten percent of expenditure. In 1995 grants totalling £12,701 were made in a total expenditure of £90,926.

One overseas project which St. Mary's continued to support was that in Pokhara, Nepal, where Jane, the daughter of Frank Schofield, was working. Jane was with the International Nepal Fellowship, working as a physiotherapist in the government hospital in Pokhara. It was from this work that the vision developed to provide some specific help for disabled children and their families, and this led to the founding of the Community Based Rehabilitation Service (CBRS) project. It was registered as a Non-Governmental Organisation in Pokhara in 1995. In 2008 a new charity - Western Nepal Disability Trust (WNDT) - was registered in the UK to provide more sustainable support to CBRS. The Trust channels donations as well as carrying out some other fundraising activities. Money from PCC donations, some of the proceeds from monthly Afternoon Teas and individual donations continue to be sent to Pokhara. This support is practically helpful and valued, as is the ongoing prayer support. [From 1988 until 2008 a total of £11,280 was sent to help there.]

In 1993 a Lay Canon of the Cathedral, Elaine Appelbee, was made responsible for carrying out a Social Survey of Parishes in the Bradford Diocese. The survey was concerned with work that the churches do in their communities. At the same time a significant event occurred in Burley. This was the closure of Scalebor Park Hospital. In the considerations which followed in Burley, it was decided that St. Mary's should try to respond to the needs of former patients now living in the village. This led to the decision to provide a place where people could call in for 'a cuppa and a chat' and allow the Church to 'create a presence in the centre of the village'. A small group was charged by the PCC to look at the possibility of using the Parish Room more effectively for this purpose. For various reasons it was

38. The first Parish Office and Open Door, in Station Road, from 1996.

thought that it was not really suitable, and there was a desire to involve the ecumenical Churches Together in Burley and Menston[92]. Unfortunately this group had no legal power to be responsible for such an undertaking. Then, mercifully, former shop premises in Station Road owned by the Jepson family became available and were offered on a rental contract as a Parish Office. St. Mary's in taking up the tenancy used this opportunity to extend the use of the building and to house the project there. A Steering Group from Churches Together was invited to plan and develop a Village Centre. They named it the Open Door. After some work was done on the building, the Parish Office and the Open Door project commenced activities in February

1996. The Bishop of Bradford came to give it his blessing.

A year later Judy Taylor, giving a report on behalf of the Steering Group to the Annual Parochial Church meeting said:

> The numbers using Open Door speak for themselves – in an
> average week, just over a hundred people come through the
> door. Many people call in for all sorts of reasons and, initially,
> a lot of these people were connected with the churches but
> gradually word is spreading and people are calling in simply to
> chat – which is where it all started. There are also people who
> have problems and are glad of a listening ear and a safe place
> where they can talk things through and perhaps be pointed in a
> direction where they can receive professional help[93].

The helpers at the centre formed a rota of attendance and were drawn from the different churches in Burley. Soon after the above report was given, the Citizens Advice Bureau in Otley was given funding to do Outreach Work, and started advice sessions on Tuesday mornings in the Open Door. The building housed the Parish Office where office equipment including computing and photocopying enabled a loyal band of volunteers to carry out administrative duties essential for the smooth running of St. Mary's.

During the first year of Peter's ministry in Burley, he was ably assisted by the curate Rev Di Halliday. In January1994 the Measure for the Ordination of Women to the priesthood at last gained the Royal Assent. There had been much concern that, before the Measure could be accepted by the Ecclesiastical Committee of the Houses of Parliament, adequate provision should be made for those clergy who were conscientiously opposed to the Measure. Financial arrangements had to made for stipendiary ministers who would feel forced to leave the Church of England. These matters were dealt with so that Parishes could, if they wished, opt out of having women priests and designated Bishops could oversee their needs. The former Lord Bishop of Durham, David Jenkins, wrote in his account of the discussions leading up to the vote:

> After a great deal of pretty agonizing discussion in the
> House of Bishops, A Draft Priests (Ordination of Women)

Measure was put to the General Synod on the morning of
10ᵗʰ December 1992 at 10 a.m...It....authorized the ordina-
tion of women...
After much debate *the time to vote arrived. The Archbishop*
advised the chamber that the vote must be received without
comment. He asked us to stand for a minute or two of
silence, said a prayer, and sent the members of Synod out to
vote by Houses – that is, Bishops, Clergy, and then Laity.
The procedure required that for the measure to succeed,
each House had to vote by a two thirds majority in favour of
it. The vote came out as:

	Ayes	*Noes*
Bishops	*39*	*13*
Clergy	*176*	*74*
Laity	*169*	*82*

This meant that technically the measure was through ......In
practice the vote represented a firm majority of the Synod as
a whole.
Looking back at it ten years later, Jenkins thought that the whole affair and
the fuss and emotion it generated seemed to verge on the absurd. He
thought that few people outside the churches could understand what all the
fuss was about[94].

The Diocese of Bradford, knowing that there was some disagreement with
the Measure, went ahead with arrangements for the ordination of women
for May 1994. In Burley, plans were made before Di Halliday was
ordained priest, to prevent a rift in the congregation. Notices were given
ahead of services indicating who would be presiding at the Eucharist so
that no one would feel excluded. This arrangement lasted for one year, as
Di Halliday then accepted an appointment to be curate at Harden parish in
September1995. It was also in 1995 that a woman was appointed as a
churchwarden. Irene Exley was elected as assistant churchwarden at the
Annual Meeting in April 1995. She was to support Paul Evans, newly
elected as churchwarden in 1994, and Keith Dale, continuing from 1992.

Rev Peter Sutcliffe's responsibilities increased when in October 1997 he was licensed to be Rural Dean of Otley. The Deanery consists of fourteen parishes, Otley, Burley, Menston, Ben Rhydding, Ilkley St. Margaret, Ilkley All Saints, Addingham, Guiseley with Esholt, Yeadon and Rawdon, Leathley, Farnley, Fewston and Weston/Denton. Peter's appointment was for five years to 2002 and required him to oversee the welfare of the clergy in all the parishes, and to act as a liaison between the parishes and the Bishop. Canon Denis Rutt continued to assist in the parish until 1999 before retiring southwards to be nearer his family. The parish was fortunate again when Canon Malcolm Emmel came to reside in Burley in 1998, after retiring from his posts as Rector of Bedale and priest-in-charge of Leeming in North Yorkshire. He had been an honorary canon of Ripon Cathedral, and had served the Church in the Alaskan region of Canada, before returning in 1966 to livings in the Ripon Diocese. He was licensed to officiate as a retired priest in the Bradford Diocese from 1998.

Major changes in the school system of the Bradford Metropolitan District took place during Peter's time in Burley, with the Educational Review of 1998. This heralded the end of Middle Schools in the whole of the Bradford district. Burley's Middle School was to close in 2000 and all primary aged children (4 to 11) would be taught in two schools. The question was which school buildings would be used. It was announced at the end of March 1998 that the old school buildings on Aireville Terrace would be closed. The new primary schools would be situated on Langford Lane in the former Middle School buildings and on Sandholme Drive in the Burley and Woodhead First School buildings. There was to be a change of status. The two First Schools had been Church of England Controlled Schools, from then on only one of them, Burley and Wood-head, was to be so designated. Some villagers would have preferred both schools to continue to have a formal Church connection, arguing that this would be less divisive. Many older villagers had been educated at the Aireville Terrace school, remembering it as the National School before 1950 and as a Church school since then. Some of the dismay was compounded by the fact that the school was celebrating its centenary at the time its closure was announced.

However Bradford insisted, for there was a delicate balance to be achieved in terms of the overall number of children in Church of England schools in the Authority. The Diocese wanted to have a Church Secondary School in Bradford which they had not had before and some primary school closures were inevitable. This had led to the conclusion that Aireville Terrace School, like others with older buildings, should be closed. The outcome was that the Langford Lane School became Burley Oaks County Primary School and the Sandholme Drive School was to become Burley and Woodhead Church of England Controlled Primary School. Both sets of buildings needed extensive changes and they were opened as primary schools in September 2000. For the most part, staff in the two First Schools continued to work in the new schools augmented by former Middle School personnel. Glynne Edwards, the headteacher at the Aireville Terrace School, and former PCC secretary, retired, but Mrs Sue Adsett, headteacher at Burley and Woodhead continued in charge of the new primary school there. Mrs Julie Speight replaced her in 2003. A former Bradford Middle School headteacher, Roy Pallas, was appointed head of Burley Oaks Primary School.

The Bradford Diocese was the sole landowner of the major part of the site of the Aireville Terrace School. Fortunately a strip of land alongside Aireville Terrace was held in trust by the Diocese for St. Mary's. It had been used for allotments during the Second World War and more recently was the site of the school canteen and some temporary classrooms. Since the war this land had been rented separately by the Education Authority and every five years or so there had been protracted negotiations about the lease, which provided useful annual income to the church. When the whole site was sold to the developers, who built the Trinity Mews residences, a part of the proceeds amounting to £675,897 was held in trust by the Diocese for community use by St. Mary's. The amount became a valuable source of money to finance the design and building of a new Parish Centre in Station Road. Initially it had been a cause of concern for the Vicar, who was anxious about the way people in Burley might interpret the closure as a gain for the Church and not for the whole community.

Preparations for Millennium celebrations also occurred as the change in the schools was taking place. Churches Together agreed to distribute candles to every household in the village and an invitation to an open air service in celebration of the Millennium in the village cricket field at midnight on 31st December 1999. Alison Sutcliffe and Caroline Jones collaborated to produce a colourful calendar which illustrated the history of Burley over a thousand years. The Community Council also contributed to the festivities with a bonfire and firework display and presented every school age child with a commemorative mug. Churches Together led by the Christian Aid committee, particularly Mary Wood, got in touch with Jon Snow, the Channel Four TV news reader, and his 'On the Line' Millennium Project. Mary visited Mali in West Africa as part of the project and as a result Burley became linked with the village of Tereli in Mali. The village has continued to support the people of Tereli with funds for particular schemes such as well digging, school buildings and a maternity unit. Zakari Saye, a son of the village chief, came to Burley bringing gifts and thanks from his people. These included a ceremonial stick which can be seen in a glass case in the Burley Library. Zakari was hoping to become a medical student at the time and some of the support Burley was giving enabled him to embark on his studies.

39. Zakari Saye presenting Bruce Speed (then Chairman of Burley Community Council) with the ceremonial stick in 2001.
Picture from Wharfedale Newspapers

The Anglican liturgy received a modern boost with the publication at the end of 2000 of *Common Worship: Services and Prayers for the Church of England. It brought together the rich inheritance of the past and the very best of our contemporary forms of worship*[95]. The lectionary in this service book was based on *The New Revised Standard Version of the Bible,* published in 1995, which itself marked attempts to provide readers with a contemporary and accessible version of the Scriptures. Order One for the Eucharist was adopted from *Common Worship* and since the new service book was also published via the internet, it was easy to download and print off service sheets for each season. The readings for Sunday worship could also be downloaded which made the printing of them on the weekly newsheets possible. Further a new setting for the Eucharist, called *The Burley Mass,* was introduced for the choir and congregation in 2000. In 1997 Peter had introduced a non-eucharistic service, which he called Open House, on the second Sunday of each month, in an attempt to widen the appeal of the Church to families in Burley.

Music continued to be an important part of church worship, and the choir a vital element in that. The annual report for 1999 noted that the choir numbered fourteen boy trebles and eleven lower voices. All the boys had opportunities to achieve Royal School of Church Music awards and in that year Chris Wood and Tim Sutcliffe gained St. Nicholas awards following external examinations. Special thanks were given to those supporting the boys behind the scenes, notably Betty and Jennifer Carson. A proposal to have a separate girls' section was noted in January 2000 but this did not proceed. Some services were accompanied by an orchestra conducted by Gill Evans, who also formed a choir of mixed voices, called St. Mary's Singers for occasional events and services in Church.

The Church community was enriched by a number of organizations feeding its social and religious needs. Sunday School continued to meet in Church, led by Audrey Birch and Annette Hattersley. The Proclaimers organized by Pam Selby had fifteen members aged eleven to sixteen. They met during the Sunday morning Eucharist and on occasional evenings, and from time to time went on visits together to other churches and places of interest. For the younger members, the Adventurers under

Audrey Birch continued but the group was finding some difficulty in attracting new recruits. The Tiny Tots for mothers and their pre-school children met in the church lounge on Wednesdays in the early afternoon. There was a theatre group which had up to twenty members and arranged visits to plays being performed in Ilkley and elsewhere. The Co-workers of Mother Theresa, a group of ladies who met on a monthly basis, organized the sending of clothing and blankets to India, Eastern Europe and to Buttershaw in Bradford. A committee of women met regularly to organize funds for the Children's Society and they organized the very popular Christingle service[96] each year as well as other fund raising events in the village. Others helped the Christian Aid committee, arranged flowers for the Church, and created banners. An Education Group organized talks on topical subjects such as human sexuality, drugs, bereavement and other Faiths. The meetings were accompanied by a supper with surplus funds being given to charities and other ventures. For instance support was given to Stephen Exley and Sharon Hattersley when they visited the Diocese of South West Virginia representing our Diocese.

The Mothers' Union celebrated their centenary in 1998 for which they had a new banner designed, placing it in an exhibition case on the south wall of the church. At this time they had fifty five members, with most attending the afternoon meetings on Wednesdays. Others attended Thursday evening meetings with the Ladies' Group, which was by now the successor to the Young Wives. The programmes of these groups included social activities and talks on topical subjects. They gave financial support to numerous charities such as the Overseas World Wide Fund, for which members had collecting boxes. Outings

40. Mothers' Union Banner.

135

were also arranged for example to Ampleforth Abbey in 1997, and to Bishopthorpe Palace in 1998.

The parish was not only ably served by its Vicar, Peter, and his assistants Canon Denis Rutt and Canon Malcolm Emmel up to the millennium, but also by a team of churchwardens, the treasurer, verger and the Parochial Church Council. During Peter's incumbency, Ian Walsh, Keith Dale , Paul Evans and Mark Selby served as church wardens up to 2000. Pip Hayes continued as Treasurer throughout and this was not an easy task for ongoing increases in the Parish Share made it necessary to keep careful check on expenditure and reserves. Budgets were usually made showing a deficit of income against expenditure. Fortunately the congregation remained relatively generous. Raymond Gill continued as Verger, a post to which the PCC had appointed him in March 1978, when he ceased to act as Lay Reader. The PCC secretarial duties during Peter's ministry were taken by Linda Hefferon, who had been appointed after Arthur Woodhead resigned in 1991. Judith Hird followed Linda in 1995 and Shirley Burns took over from Judith in 1999. Deanery Synod members at this time included Betty Bentley, Desmond Lewis-Ogden, Nancy Midgely, and Isobel Somerfield, who also represented the Deanery on the Diocesan Synod. Among those who were elected to the PCC during Peter's incumbency, several had served the congregation for a number of years already, such as Christine Clark, Janet Squire, Glynis Mowat, Kelvin Newberry, Bill Pickles, Liz Wilson, Pam Sowman, Audrey Birch and Sue Settle. Sue, a teacher at Burley and Woodhead school, had been much involved with Sunday School and Youth work, and had organized numerous social activities. Sadly she was not to see in the new millennium as she died after a long illness in 1997.

In the year 2000 the PCC agreed to the setting up of workshops to look at future patterns of worship and the whole mission of the Church. The task was given the title *The Way Ahead.* The originator and coordinator was Enid Feather, a member of the PCC who had recently gained a Master's Degree in Health Administration and recognized that her knowledge could be useful also to the Church. Enid suggested to the Vicar that St. Mary's needed a strategy. With Peter's support *The Way Ahead* was formulated. The Vicar started the process with a sermon outlining different models and approaches to church and church worship to stimulate discussion. There were three workshops, which were followed by plenary discussions to which all members of the congregation were invited. Many members of the congregation attended at least one of these sessions. Workshop One was concerned with the question 'Where are we now?' Its report concluded that we are a church with no walls, but recognized that others may sense that there are barriers to membership. If so we needed to find ways of helping them to build their relationship with us and with God. Workshop Two took as its question 'Where do we want to be?' Here the conclusions were that we should help the regular members of the congregation to be more focused in their worship, to be mindful of the duties of Christian Stewardship, to be involved in the life of the community, and to be actively concerned for the needs of others. Workshop Three then looked at the future and faced the question How are we going to get there?' Its conclusions were: First, there should be much more discussion of our faith and its meaning, in house groups and occasional retreats or away days, and more variety in our worship. Second, we should contact people when they come to church for funerals, weddings, baptisms and Christmas services offering a welcome to the other services and to meetings of organizations connected to our Church. Third, in our involvement with the community we should be more proactive and use all existing lines of communications for instance through Churches Together and the village Schools. Fourth, we should keep abreast of the world beyond the parish, its problems and its needs. The plenary sessions which followed the workshops underlined these objectives and accepted a Mission Statement for our Church:

> *A community rooted in worship and prayer,*
> *striving to grow in faith and love;*
> *serving our community, our purpose is to bring others to Him.*

Generally we can say that St. Mary's moved from the 20th Century with a continuing sense of wanting to live by the two commandments which Jesus gave us: *Thou shalt love the Lord thy God* and *Thou shalt love Thy*

Neighbour as Thyself. The Church's worship gave regular and strong emphasis to the Eucharist and the Sunday sermon, and with greater lay participation every opportunity was given to all members of the congregation to consider and renew their commitment. The continuing work of its organizations, such as those mentioned above, the links with other Churches and the Open Door in Station Road gave clear messages of concern for the whole community and the world at large. Such Church initiatives were not always recognized, however, and many of the growing population in the village appeared indifferent, except perhaps when they wished to celebrate their rites of passage.

41. Gill Evans conducting the orchestra, with Joan Ogden
at the key board.

CHAPTER SEVEN

THE NEW MILLENNIUM

St. Mary's mission statement: 'A community rooted in worship and prayer, striving to grow in faith and love; serving the community, our purpose is to bring others to Jesus.[97]

Though the world has changed much since Dr. Black ministered to Burley, the mission of the Church has altered only slightly. It was summed up then in that quotation which heads the Preface. The 1864 statement shows perhaps more urgency and less desire for ecumenical relations than our present one, but we hope today, like Charles Ingham Black, to bring others to Jesus. In this final chapter we can only point to recent developments and changes. It will be up to later historians to make a more comprehensive assessment of St.Mary's in the new millennium.

Peter Sutcliffe gave a full summary of worship and purpose at St. Mary's in 2001 in a letter to the Bishop of Bradford describing the parish and the church, in preparation for the ordination of a deacon who was coming to work in Burley.

The worship at St. Mary's is primarily Eucharistic. Average attendances are given in brackets. We use the Book of Common Prayer at 8 a.m.[30], and from November will be using Rite 1 from Common Worship at 9.45a.m. [140]. We use the Book of Common Prayer for Evensong on Sundays [5] – once a month this is fully choral [30]. There is a mid week Eucharist on Thursdays [20]. Once a month the 9.45 a.m. Eucharist is replaced with Open House, a non-eucharistic service, which has attracted new people to the church in recent years. The Eucharist is celebrated once a month at the nursing home next to the church, and in a sheltered housing complex. Members of the congregation take the sacrament to the sick and housebound after the Sunday Eucharist.

The congregation is socially, intellectually and theologically mixed in a very creative way. The prevailing churchmanship is central, sometimes becoming gently catholic, other times gently evangelical. Vestments are worn, the sacrament is reserved. In addition to the New English Hymnal, we use material from Mission Praise and from the Iona and Taize communities. In 1999 there were 31 baptisms, 21 weddings and 31 funerals and cremations.

The church has a recently restored pipe organ and a portable keyboard. There is a male choir of some 26 voices, and a mixed auxiliary choir, the St. Mary's Singers. Our music is further enriched by a recorder ensemble and a small orchestra, both of which play regularly. The vicar is assisted by two Readers and a recently retired priest. Lay

42. Paul Allan (end left) with the Vicar (back row centre) and Choir in 2000.

*people play a vital part in our life, and take initiatives
easily.*

Peter also added:
> *There are three other Christian churches in the village,
> URC, Methodist and Roman Catholic......The clergy meet
> together regularly. There are frequent ecumenical services,
> we distribute promotional material together, and jointly run
> a "drop-in" centre* [the Open Door] *which is based in the
> same building as the Parish Office.*

The parish gained an assistant curate in 2001 when Dr. Roger Brookes
came to serve as Deacon after ordination that year. Roger had been a
consultant anaesthetist, but in his fifties his vocation changed, and he came
to Burley to learn how to cure souls. During the early months of 2002 he
had extra duties as Peter Sutcliffe had leave of absence through illness.
Roger was priested in 2002 and stayed until the summer of 2003, when he
was appointed Priest in Charge at Denholme, Harden and Wilsden. Canon
Malcolm Emmel has continued to assist throughout the first decade of the
new millennium. More recently another retired priest, Rev. Chris Hayward
has come to live in the village, and though he has some Diocesan duties he
also assists at Services.

Peter recovered from his illness in 2002, but in April 2003 announced his
resignation to take up an incumbency at St. Andrew's Yeadon. The
Diocese closed St. Andrew's in 2006 because it was not thought viable,
and Peter then became Vicar of Lightcliffe, near Halifax. In 2009 he was
installed as Vicar of four parishes in Northumberland.

Rev Michael Burley was presented to the Parish and installed by the
Bishop of Bradford, the Right Reverend David James, as incumbent in
November 2003. Mark Selby and Hilary Walsh, as Parish representatives,
had advised the Bishop on the kind of appointment the Parish wanted and
took part in the interviewing process of candidates who had applied to an
Advertisement in *The Church Times*. Michael, a Yorkshireman born in

1958, studied at Ridley Hall, Cambridge after a short career in finance. He was made deacon in 1989 and priested in 1990. His first curacy was in Scarborough, and the second in Drypool, East Yorkshire, where quite soon he became Team Vicar. He was appointed Vicar of St. Michael's, Sutton, in Humberside in 1997 where he served for six years before coming to Burley. The old vicarage in Cornmill Lane, to which he came with his wife Liz and family, was seen as increasingly dilapidated. The PCC in 2005 agreed that there ought to be a better house and asked the Diocese to arrange for a replacement. This eventually led to the family taking up residence at 21, Southfield Road at the end of 2006.

The decade has seen the death of some long serving and loyal members of the congregation; John Squire died in 2001, Pip Hayes in September 2004, Audrey Birch in April 2005, Frank Newbould in March 2006 and

Raymond Gill in March 2009. These deaths entailed changes for the Church and its organisations. The Choir lost a valuable tenor in John Squire, and a notable bass (and historian) in Frank Newbould; the Sunday School lost its long term leader and the Church a verger. Pip Hayes had been the treasurer until his death, a post which was then ably filled by Duncan Watts. Liz Burley had taken

43. Rev. Michael Burley and his wife Liz.

over the leadership of the Sunday School during Audrey Birch's illness and continued to do so until 2008, when Lizzie Reynolds took her place. The position of Verger has not been refilled, but the necessary duties are covered by a number of volunteers.

The Choir did not recruit other men to replace John Squire and Frank Newbould. George Smith nobly sang until his death in 2008 and younger singers in turn left for jobs or higher education. Fewer boys came forward and the attractions of Sunday football lured them away from Church on Sunday mornings. Those that remained gave of their best under the leadership of Paul Allan, who had been the organist and choir master from 1990. His inspired organ playing did not however attract the kind of singers of his earlier years. Another Hymn Book, *Complete Anglican, Hymns Old and New*, was adopted in place of *New English Hymnal*. The money for it was donated by the family of Alice Holderness, former leader of the Mothers' Union and widow of Neville, choir member and former treasurer for the Christian Stewardship committee. Paul Allan retired in

44. St. Mary's Singers on the occasion of an evening of African religious songs.

Paul Evans

143

2008. The St. Mary's Singers, a mixed choir both in age and gender, led by Gill Evans, provide choral support for the congregation on special occasions, notably at Christmas and Easter and for Open House services. They have also sung at a number of themed services, including an African evening and a performance, with instrumental support, of *Joseph and his Amazing Technicolour Dreamcoat*. The Vicar's own musical skills and enthusiasm, not to mention those of Liz Burley, Dorrie Clarke and Claire Richards, contributed to the success of these events.

The lack of an organist led to the suspension of Choral Evensong. On Sunday evenings there is a regular gathering for prayer or a healing service and occasionally a Churches Together service. The most recent statistics, those for 2008, show that the normal Sunday attendance was 123 adults and 34 under sixteens. Christmas Day communicants numbered 209 and Easter, 208. There were 37 baptisms, 12 weddings and 16 funerals in Church.

In 2001 a new Measure concerning Churchwardens was agreed by General Synod and Parliament which introduced limited periods of office and confirmed their role:

> *They are elected by the people in the parish, work collaboratively with the incumbent and, finally, act as the bishop's lay officers in the parish, for the people, with the priest, on behalf of the bishop....Every parish, every parish priest and every bishop needs good churchwardens. With rare exception, we have them. In passing this Measure, the House will be giving them support and help in the work they do in this historic office. I hope that the Measure will have approval today and I commend it to the House[98].*

The first woman to be elected as Churchwarden of St. Mary's was Janet Squire in 2004. She was joined by Gail Boole the following year, after Duncan Watts had become the Treasurer. Both of them remain in post at the time of writing (See Appendix 3 for a full list of Churchwardens).

The PCC during this first decade of the new millennium is, as Peter Sutcliffe commented in 2001, a happy one. 'Its members contribute easily and willingly to discussions. We vote only on those things which we are required by law to vote on, and otherwise proceed, or not, on the basis of consensus. The Vicar does not always get his own way!' Tracy Dale continued as PCC secretary until 2005, when Mark Selby took on the role. The annual request from the Diocese to contribute a major slice of the Church's income as its Parish Share, tends to be a major item for discussion. The Christian Stewardship committee, now chaired by Nigel Cottam, receives considerable support from over one hundred regular givers, and with tax relief on covenanted donations this yielded an income of about £100,000 in 2008. The Parish Share, however, has taken an increasing proportion of the income of the Church over the decade and this has led one of the members of the PCC to make a comparative study of parish shares across English Dioceses. This revealed that we in the Bradford Diocese tend to be asked to find comparatively more per giver than in other dioceses. A more equitable situation across the dioceses in this country would be welcome. The study was published as an article in *The Church Times* in May 2009, and it is hoped that this will widen the discussion and achieve some benefit (See appendix 4).

Another issue over the decade has been the question of whether we in the Otley Deanery can continue to have the same number of ministers and parishes. This has not been resolved, but as a move in the direction of having parishes working together, St. Mary's Burley and St. John's Menston are now sharing an assistant curate. Rev. Ernest Lennon was ordained Deacon in 2008 and was appointed to the parishes, to provide support while the Vicars of the two parishes, Michael Burley and Ruth Yeomans give some of their time to Diocesan work with candidates applying and preparing for ordination.

45. Rev. Ernest Lennon

Ecumenical activity continues through work of *Churches Together* which includes all the churches of Burley and Menston. A series of Lent Lectures is held in the Roman Catholic Church each year. There is an annual walk of witness on Good Friday between Menston and Burley, and joint publicity for village services at Christmas and Easter. Lent Lunches on each Friday of Lent are provided by volunteers organized by Susannah Shaw and served in Burley Methodist Church Fellowship Room. Funds raised are given to Christian Aid, whose committee includes members from all the churches. Regular Christian Aid meetings take place in Salem

46. Rev Michael Burley and Dr. Zakari Saye, June 2009
Photo: Mary Wood

Church in Burley. In 2009 Dr. Zakari Saye visited Burley again having gained his medical degree in Mali. He wanted to thank Christian Aid and members of the Burley Tereli Friendship Trust for all the help that was and is directed by them to his village, his country and his studies. Another example of the ecumenical work is the development of a Fair Trade policy with some of the businesses in Burley, led by Keith Dale (Chairman of the Burley Parish Council), Janet Squire and Mary Wood. Burley now has "Fair Trade Village Status". St. Mary's covenant with Burley Methodist Church continues to flourish. The new minister there, Rev. Timothy

47. Zakari Saye with members of the Burley Christian Aid Committee during his
visit in June 2009.   Photo by Wharfedale Newspapers.

Perkins, has celebrated the Eucharist in St. Mary's and Michael Burley has
officiated similarly in the Methodist Church. The two churches are also
sharing a Youth Worker, Matt Wright, both contributing to his salary. Matt
works with the Revelation Group, or 'REV', at St. Mary's, and with the
Cyber Café at the Methodist Church. There is some crossover of
membership. 'REV' was started some years ago by Pam Selby, and further
developed by Nik Legge who now works with Matt. The Methodist
Church was extensively refurbished at the beginning of the decade. Its
gallery has been converted into a large meeting room and offices
accessible from both stairs and a lift, whilst the ground floor has been

divided into a worship area and a fellowship area. A movable partition divides the two allowing for larger congregations. The fellowship area is provided with a well equipped kitchen and other services, very suitable for meetings of small and medium sized groups.

There was much discussion of change to St. Mary's buildings in the early part of the decade with some serious architectural research into various options. Much of this has been set aside to allow for what has been the major achievement. One of the options was for a new building on the site of the Parish Office and Open Door on Station Road. The continuing need for a presence in the centre of the village made this the first and most important goal. John Spencer and a small group of PCC members formulated ideas for a Parish Centre project. The sum of money held in trust for community use by the Diocese, resulting from the sale of land on Aireville Terrace after the closure of the school, was sufficient to enable the scheme to go ahead. A leading firm, Ellis Williams Architects of

48. The opening of St. Mary's Parish Centre in Station Road by the Bishop of Bradford in May 2007.

Liverpool, was commissioned to design a modern building for a Parish Centre. When planning permission was given and builders contracted to do the job, work started in 2006. The site was somewhat constricted, but fortunately the house next door, at no.1, Grange Road, went on sale. Its purchase by the Church gave the builders much better access to the site. The functions of the Parish Office and Open Door were also able to continue there during the building. Inevitable delays meant that the original target date for completion in March was not met.

On 20th May 2007, with the Bishop of Bradford committed to perform the opening ceremony, a more or less complete Centre was formally blessed and commissioned for use by the community. St. Mary's Parish Centre now provides space for virtually non-stop activities, including the Open Door, the Meeting Place (coffee bar), Coffee Mornings most Saturdays, art, ballet and fitness classes, ante and post natal classes, and a well equipped Parish Office. When the Open Door started up in the new building, Bob and Liz Wilson continued to organize the volunteers who welcome and serve its visitors. A pleasant garden opens out to the south of the building. Paul Evans, a former churchwarden recently retired from his full-time employment, took on the task of voluntarily managing the Centre. With teams of volunteers in the office and Open Door, the Centre has become a real success. Hire charges paid for use of the rooms are meeting the running costs of the Centre. A logo for the Church and the Centre was designed by Jaqui Poncelet in partnership with the architects of the building. It combines symbols of thorns and roses, representing death and resurrection, helping to convey the Christian message of hope.

49. The new logo.

The office is the main contact point and communication centre for St. Mary's. Weekly

149

newsheets, Service sheets and the monthly Parish Magazine are produced there. The editorship of the magazine has passed through some able hands during the decade, Frank Schofield, Adrian Allsop and more recently Joyce Russell. The Church website

50. The Parish Room, in a yard off Station Road

which was first opened in Peter Sutcliffe's incumbency has been developed and now attractively carries much information about the

51. The last PCC coffee morning in the Parish Room.

Church, the congregation and its links to the wider world.
(www.burleyparishchurch.org.uk)

The completion of the new Parish Centre meant that the Parish Room, which had been the Church's property in the middle of Burley since the beginning of the twentieth century, was no longer needed. This ancient building, possibly a former Grammar School and more certainly a farm in the nineteenth century, was sold in 2008 to a firm of environmental consultants for use as an office. For many years, as we have noted previously, it had been used by the Church and other village organisations for meetings. Many will remember the Saturday fund raising coffee mornings held there. The house at no.1, Grange Road, was also sold, being bought by the Diocese as a home for Rev Ernest Lennon and his family.

The Church itself has had some work done to make the Parish Lounge more serviceable, though a scheme for enlarging it has been put aside until the financial situation can be reconsidered. The path from the gate on Cornmill Lane to the main entrance has been graded and steps into the Church removed so that there is wheelchair access into the nave. A board listing all the incumbents of the Parish has been added to the porch. It was made at the "mouseman" workshop in Kilburn. The plans for making a 'side chapel' in place of some of the pews caused some argument. This was proposed by the Parish Welcome Group, an ad hoc group of PCC members and others from the congregation, working on a document submitted by our former curate, Rev. Eileen McLean. She had visited churches across the country and felt that many lacked any sense of welcome.

The Welcome Group grew out of one of the four working groups reporting to the PCC. These Groups were set up to reflect on and advance the purposes set out in the Mission Statement. They are: 'Striving to grow in faith and love', 'Sharing in worship and prayer', 'Serving the community' and 'Leading others to Christ'. They feed into and recommend decisions to the PCC with regard to links with the Schools in the village, the pattern of worship in the Church and activities with the village and wider community. The Serving the community group, for instance, recommends the annual grants to be given to agencies and charities here and abroad, such as those in Pokhara, Nepal and the Peace Centre for the Blind in Jerusalem. There are many other groups actively trying to meet the needs

52. St. Mary's nave and chancel, July 2009.

of the congregation such as Bible and Christian Reading groups, Sunday School, Revelation, Mothers' Union, Ladies' Group and Theatre Group. One which is called "Open the Book" sprang out of a Deanery initiative by Judith Wigley based on the *Lion Storytellers' Bible* by Bob Hartman. She put together the materials and props and the first project took place in Burley and Woodhead C.E. Primary School with Susannah Shaw, Sue and Vernon Whelan, Barbara Schofield and Kelvin Newberry taking part. Since then it has undertaken projects in the other schools. For instance they have taken two one hour sessions at each of the Burley Oaks, Burley and Woodhead and Ghyll Royd Schools, in which 'whole of the Bible' stories have been conveyed to Key stage two pupils. The response has been heartening.

The perplexity of the modern world continues of course to make the practice of our faith and mission difficult. It was probably no more easy in the days of Charles Ingham Black but it seems to be more complex in the twenty first century. We are more aware of the continuing challenges to the basis of our beliefs from other faiths and non-believers. The speed of communications by telephone, satellite and the internet makes it impossible to conceive of 'loving our neighbour as ourselves' as anything other than a global responsibility. There are estimated to be in 2009 nearly seven billion people living on the Earth. We have to be concerned for the effect of humans on our world, its environment, its climate and its resources. Continuing conflicts between peoples and groups of different nationalities, ethnicities and political and religious beliefs make our task more and more difficult. We must not let our faith and our membership of the Anglican Communion restrict our understanding of and our love for our neighbours. In the Bradford Diocese we have of course almost a microcosm of the world and its peoples from whom we can learn much about helping and loving our neighbours.

Like David Jenkins we would like to conclude by encouraging present and future Christians to be interested not only in the past but also in the future. Among many other events there will be a bi-centenary of St. Mary's in 2043 and we hope it will go well. As David Jenkins said: 'Oh, come *on* all ye faithful! We are called to join in God's amazing agenda of unending love with all the grace, guts and intellectual, spiritual, moral energy and insight we can muster …[in the conviction] that God will multiply our efforts in ever more far-reaching ways if we will just take the risk'[99].

53. A Good Friday Ecumenical Walk of Witness in Station Road, Burley.

Photo: Peter Sutcliffe

APPENDIX ONE
LIST OF INCUMBENTS, CHAPLAINS, PERPETUAL CURATES AND VICARS

We have taken the list as published on the Board in the Church Porch. This is compiled from information contained in Black's *Historical Memorials*. David Nealy in his history suggests others, but without clear evidence.

CHAPLAINS OR CURATES FROM 1664

1664	Thomas Harrison
1670	Samuel Ward
1680	John Wack
1687	Richard Vitty
1699	John Vitty
1708	Christopher Holt
1723	Thomas Lister
1745	Thomas Dawson
1745	Thomas Wilkinson
1758	Edmund Beeston (also Vicar of Ilkley)
1778	George Benson
1800	John Chapman
1813	William Smith
1835	Edmund Hodgkinson
1848	Frederick Langhorne
1852	Hugh Robinson
1854	William F. Black

1855	Charles Ingham Black (received title of Vicar in 1868)

Thereafter the incumbents are known as Vicars

1896	Ralph P. Stedman
1902	Eric R. Buckley
1921	William Crawford Allan
1936	Edmund Neville Pedley
1955	John Beardsmore
1969	Donald B. Aldred
1984	John H. Tidy
1993	Peter Sutcliffe
2003	Michael Burley

The Board in the porch on which these names are listed was supplied by the Thompson workshops in Kilburn, North Yorkshire and was given in memory of Pip and Jay Hayes, who gave considerable service to St. Mary's from the 1960s to the Millennium. Pip outlived Jay and he died in 2004.

APPENDIX TWO

CONSECRATION OF ST. MARY'S CHURCH, BURLEY-IN-WHARFEDALE.

FROM *THE LEEDS INTELLIGENCER*, 24TH JUNE 1843

On Monday last, the Right Rev. the Lord Bishop of Ripon consecrated the newly-erected Church to be called the Church or Chapel of St. Mary the Blessed Virgin at Burley. The Lord Bishop was received at the gates of the Church-yard, by the Vicar of Otley, the Incumbent and the Curate of Burley, and a numerous body of Clergymen, in their surplices, the Churchwardens of Otley and Burley, the members of the Building Committee, and other functionaries, and was escorted into the porch at the West End, where the Vicar of Otley presented to the Right Rev. Prelate, the petition of himself and other parishioners of Otley and Burley, humbly praying that his Lordship would be pleased to consecrate the Church and Burying Ground adjoining. The Lord Bishop handed the petition to Edward John Teale, Esq., of Leeds, the Registrar of the Archdeaconry of Craven, and acting Registrar of the Diocese of Ripon, by whom the document was read aloud. When the reading had been concluded, the Bishop said – "I am ready to consecrate the Church and Burial Ground, according to the prayer of this Petition."

His Lordship and the Clergy then proceeded slowly down the centre aisle of the Church towards the Communion table, his Lordship and the Clergy alternately repeating the ten verses of the 24th Psalm. The Bishop took his usual place at the north side of the altar, the Rev Joshua Hart, Vicar of Otley, going to the south side, and the Rev. Edmund Hodgkinson, Incumbent of Burley, to the reading desk. The Right Rev. Prelate, then read the appointed service of Consecration, praying as well for those that may be married therein, as, for those who may be baptised, or confirmed, or who may communicate therein. At the conclusion of the accustomed consecration prayers, the Bishop resumed his seat at the north side of the Communion table. Mr. E. J. Teale, as acting Registrar of the Diocese, then read the Sentence of Consecration.

It began by reciting that it had been represented unto the Lord Bishop by a Petition under the hands of Joshua Hart, clerk, Vicar of the parish of Otley in Yorkshire, in the Diocese of Ripon, Edmund Hodgkinson, clerk, Perpetual Curate of the Chapelry of Burley in the said Parish, Edmund Richardson, Clerk, Jonas

157

Whitaker, Esq., Wm. Fairbank, Esq., George Sheppard, Esq;, Thomas Fox, Joseph Whitehead, and divers other persons, inhabitants of Otley and Burley aforesaid, that the ancient Chapel of the Chapelry or Perpetual Curacy of Burley; aforesaid, being in a ruinous and dilapidated state, and insufficient for the accommodation of the inhabitants assembling therein for divine worship, the Petitioners, together with other inhabitants of Otley and Burley aforesaid, had, at their own expense, aided by subscriptions and donations, by virtue of a Licence or Faculty under the seal of the Consistory Court of York, and dated the 6th day of April, 1841, taken down and removed the said Chapel, and on or near the site thereof had erected and built upon an enlarged scale a new Church or Chapel intended to be called the Church or Chapel of St. Mary the Blessed Virgin, at Burley aforesaid; and also that the said old chapel contained, accommodation for 160 persons only, of which 130 sittings were appropriated or claimed by various persons; and that the said new Church contains 507 sittings, of which 259 are free; and further that the piece of ground formerly used as a yard to the said Chapel (delineated in the plans drawn in the margins of the Petition and of the Sentence of Consecration) contained, with the site of the new Church or Chapel, an area of 1700 yards, and was intended to be used as and for a burial ground or cemetery belonging to the said Church or Chapel; and that the said Church or Chapel was fitted up and furnished with all things needful and necessary for the due performance of divine service therein; and that the said piece of ground was sufficiently fenced in; and that the same were respectively ready for consecration; and the said Petitioners humbly prayed the Lord Bishop of Ripon that he would be pleased to consecrate and dedicate the said Church or Chapel, to set apart and separate from all common and profane uses, and to dedicate the same solemnly to the service of Almighty God, to be and remain a Church or Chapel, by the name of the Church or Chapel of St. Mary the Blessed Virgin, in Burley forever; and also that his Lordship would be pleased to consecrate and appropriate the said piece of ground so fenced as aforesaid, and surrounding the said church or chapel, as a cemetery or piece of Christian burial for the dead, as a yard to the said church or chapel: therefore, he, the said Charles Thomas, by divine permission Bishop of Ripon, did by his authority Ordinary and Episcopal, so far as in him lay, and by law he could, separate and set apart the said church or chapel from all common and profane uses whatsoever, and did dedicate the same to Almighty God and Divine Worship, and consecrate it for the celebration thereof, and did openly and publicly pronounce, decree, and declare that the same ought so to remain, separated, dedicated, and consecrated; and did pronounce and appoint the said church or chapel by the name or title of 'The Church or Chapel of St. Mary the Blessed

Virgin, at Burley' by this his Lordship's definite sentence or final decree, read and promulgated by these presents; and he did also separate and set apart the said piece of ground so fenced in as aforesaid, and surrounding the church or chapel from all common and profane uses whatsoever, and did, as far as in him lay and by law he could, assign the same as and to be a cemetery or burial place annexed to the said church or chapel, and he did dedicate and consecrate the same for that purpose, and did openly and publicly pronounce, decree and declare the same to be so assigned, separated, dedicated, and consecrated for ever, and that the same ought so to remain; by this his definite sentence of final decree, which he also made and promulgated by these presents.

The instrument was then presented to the Bishop, who signed it on the Communion Table. His Lordship then returned it to the Registrar, saying "Let the Petition and Sentence of Consecration be registered among the Muniments of the Diocese."

The Daily Morning service was then read by the Incumbent of Burley, the Bishop reading the appointed prayers after the Collect for the day and after the General Thanksgiving. The old Hundredth Psalm was then sung. The Communion Service was read by the Bishop, the Epistle being read by the Rev Joshua Hart. After the Communion, the following hymn was sung:

> Lord of Hosts, to thee we raise
> Here a house of prayer and praise;
> Thou thy people's hearts prepare
> Here to meet, for praise and prayer.
>
> Let the living here be fed
> With thy word, - the heavenly bread!
> Here, in hope of glory, blest,
> May the dead be laid to rest.
>
> Here to thee a Temple stand
> While the sea shall gird the land:
> Here reveal thy mercy sure,
> While the sun and moon endure.
>
> Hallelujah! Earth and sky

159

To the joyful sound reply!
Hallelujah! Hence ascend
Prayer and praise till time shall end!

The sermon was preached by the Lord Bishop, from Psalm cxxii v.1. "I was glad when they said unto me 'Let us go into the House of the Lord' ". His Lordship observed that the joy which the Royal Psalmist experienced when thus invited to join with the congregation of faithful men in the House of God, would be shared, in some degree at least, by those whose hearts were inclined to be moved by the same holy spirit which dictated these words; but even the advanced Christian would sometimes feel himself deeply humbled when reflection compelled him to acknowledge how wide was the interval that still separated him from that degree of religious attainment indicated by the fervent aspirations of the Royal Psalmist. David, indeed, appeared to have felt some difficulty in finding figures strong enough to express the intensity of that desire with which he longed to take part in those sacred services. The hart panting after the water brooks, and the well which the weary pilgrim found in a dry and thirsty land, scarcely served to indicate the strength of his feelings, under the influence of which he broke forth in those affecting exclamations recorded in the 84th Psalm – "How amiable are thy tabernacles, O Lord of hosts! My soul longeth, yea, even fainteth for the Courts of the Lord; my heart and my flesh crieth out for the living God." "Blessed are they that dwell in thy house; they will be still praising thee," "For a day in thy Courts is better than a thousand, I had rather be a doorkeeper in the house of my God, than to dwell in the tents of wickedness."

Many of those who heard him (the Bishop said) might never, probably, experience the feelings of one who had been debarred by adverse circumstances from such privileges, and the very facilities which were afforded to them for their enjoyment might render them too little sensible of their value, and not sufficiently thankful for their uninterrupted continuance. The motives too which drew a mixed congregation together were of a very varied character. With some it was merely the force of custom that led them to the door of the sanctuary; their forefathers were wont to resort thither before them, and they had followed instinctively the same track. With others the practice originated, though it might not be confined, in the lusts of the eye and the pride of life, the desire of seeing and being seen, the pleasure of mixing in an assembly where they might hope to rid themselves for a time of the tedium that usually attends a vacant and inactive life. Some again might be drawn there by idle curiosity on occasions of special interest, instead of according to apostolic order and in conformity with the requirements of the Primitive Church. The Right Reverend Preacher then proceeded to point our the advantages of attendance on public worship, and to exhort his hearers to be constant and zealous in their attendance of the public ministrations of the Church.

The Offertory was then read by the Rev. J. Hart and the Rev. Edmund Richardson, Curate of Burley, during which the Churchwardens collected the Alms of the Congregation, towards liquidating the remaining debt on the Church. The collection amounted to £52 2s. 9½d.

The Bishop then pronounced the concluding prayer and benediction, and immediately proceeded out of the great western door to the east end of the Churchyard, where the ceremony of consecrating the burial ground was performed. The Right Rev. Prelate then returned to the Vestry in the north west corner of the Church, where his Lordship unrobed, and afterwards gave audience to several of the Clergy.

The Bishop, the Clergy, the Building Committee and several lay visitors, were then conducted to the National School, which had been licensed for the performance of Divine Worship during the rebuilding of the Church, and where a cold collation was laid out. The Rev. Edmund Hodgkinson presided, supported on his right by the Bishop, the Rev. E.M. Hall, E. J. Teale, Esq., and on his left by the Rev. Joshua Hart, the Rev. Geo. Lewthwaite, the Rev. John Snowden, &c. The Rev. Edmund Richardson officiated as Vice-Chairman.

After the repast, the health of "the Queen" and "of the Lord Bishop of the Diocese" were severally proposed and drank. The Bishop briefly responded. He trusted he need not tell them that it had been a cordial gratification to him to meet his reverend and lay friends on such an occasion. He had only just returned from London: and there seemed to be a freshness and a delight in coming at once amongst his brethren in Burley on such an occasion which was truly gratifying, especially when he saw around him so many well known friends, not only among the Clergy, but among the laity, many excellent supporters of the Church whom he recognized as having met on former and similar occasions. They were always in their places, cordially supporting the best interests of the Church, and doing what they could for the welfare of their poorer neighbours, in advancing such buildings as that they just consecrated. He could only say that it was his cordial and sincere wish and prayer that the business of that day might prove to be a continued blessing to the many inhabitant of the place. His Lordship concluded by proposing "the healths of the Vicar of Otley, and the Incumbent of Burley".

The Vicar of Otley acknowledged the compliment. "The health of the Rev. Edmund Richardson" was also proposed by the Bishop, and responded to by the Rev. Gentleman. The Bishop next proposed "the healths of Messrs Whitaker, Mitchell, and Fairbank, members of the Church Building Committee". Mr. Fairbank acknowledged the compliment, and expressed the satisfaction he had felt at seeing the erection of the Church completed, a satisfaction which had, if possible, been increased by the compliment which had just been paid to him and his colleagues on the Committee. The Rev. J. Hart proposed "the Otley and Burley Churchwardens", who had rendered good service at the Consecration that day in keeping order. Mr. Foster and Mr. Flesher, of Otley, severally returned thanks. The company then separated.

Among the Clergy and Laity present at the service on this interesting occasion we observed the Rev. Joshua Hart, Vicar of Otley; the Rev. Edmund Hodgkinson, Incumbent of Burley; the Rev. Edmund Richardson, curate of Burley; the Rev. George Lewthwaite, Vicar of Adel; the Rev. Wm. Thompson, Rector of Addingham; the Rev. John Snowden, Vicar of Ilkley; the Rev. A. Ibbotson of Rawden; the Rev, W.H. B. Stocker of Horsforth; the Rev. D. Jenkins of Pudsey; the Rev. E.M. Hall of Idle; the Rev. J. Barber of Bierley; the Rev. Thos. Newberry of Shipley; the Rev. J. W. Ridsdale of Pool and Bramhope; the Rev. J. Muncaster of Oulton; the Rev. Wm, Sherwood of St. James' Church, Bradford; the Rev. Thos. Pitts of Sowerby (late Curate of Otley); the Rev. James Campbell Holme, Curate of Otley; the Rev. Edw. Stirling Murphy, Curate of Fewston; the Rev. John Horsfall, Curate of Weston and Denton, &c. Jonas Whitaker, Esq., Burley; Francis Billam, Esq., Newall Hall; Benj. Thompson, Esq., Park Gate; William Ellis, Esq., Castlefield, Bingley; Edwin Greenwood, Esq., Keighley; John Farrar, Esq., Grove House, Pudsey; Wm. Milthorpe Maude, Esq., Knosthorpe, Leeds; James Maude, Esq., Potternewton, Leeds; George Hayward, Esq., Headingley; Edward Johnson Mitchell, Esq., Bradford; Mr. Turley, Yeadon; Mr. Walker Rawstorne, architect, Bradford, &c.

The Church is built of stone in the pointed or early English style of architecture, with a lantern and spire, and has a remarkably handsome appearance, both externally and internally. It is, moreover, a striking object to the traveler from Otley to Ilkley and Skipton, as it stands upon the highest plot of ground in the vicinity of Burley Hall It is 62 feet long by 34 feet wide, exclusive of the chancel, tower, &c., and its extreme length, externally, is 92 feet. It is warmed with hot water on the north and south sides, all glazed with ground glass. The three pointed windows at the east end are glazed with stained glass, something after the manner of "the Five Sisters", in the north transept of York Cathedral, and are the workmanship, we understand, of Mr. Wm. Wales of Newcastle upon Tyne.

The Communion table has been furnished with a neat altar cloth in crimson, and a handsome Communion Service in silver. The reading desk stands in the chancel on the north side of the altar; the pulpit is in a corresponding position on the south side. At the west end is a spacious gallery; the whole being calculated, as stated above, to seat 507 persons.

The foundation stone of the Edifice was laid on the 14th October 1841 and the erection has been completed according to the design of Mr. Walker Rawstorne, of Bradford, the architect. In the third (or last) Report of "the Society for Promoting the Increase of Church Accommodation and the Endowment of Churches in the Diocese of Ripon", it is stated that the cost of the erection is estimated at £1,773 15s. 4d.; towards which that Society had granted £300; a grant of £150 had been made by the Incorporated Society for building Churches; £989 11s. 5d. had been raised by subscriptions; and the inhabitants of Burley had gratuitously provided materials, labour, leading, &c., to the amount of £43 11s 0d.

The population of Burley at the last census was 1736.

On Monday evening, an impressive and appropriate Sermon was preached by the Rev. Hugh Stowell, of Manchester, from Luke 7 v 22, "To the poor the Gospel is preached".
The collection amounted to £18 17s. 7½d., which, together with £11, contributed by friends who were unable to attend personally, makes the collections of the day amount to £82 0s. 5d.

APPENDIX THREE
LIST OF CHURCHWARDENS IN BURLEY-IN-WHARFEDALE

1744 Joseph Dobson
1745 John Brogden
1746 Thomas Shelden
1750 William Gill
1751 Joseph Simpson
1754 Joseph Dobson
1755 Thomas Rhodes
1758 Richard Ellerbeck
1760 Joseph Hodgson
1772 Michael Stead
1773 Thomas Rhodes
1776 William Brown
1777 William Moss
1780 Michael Stead
1783 George Brumfitt
1784 Michael Stead
1786 Joseph Simpson
1789 John Simpson
1790 Thomas Hodgson
1793 John Patefield
1797 John Simpson
1801 Jonas Walker
1802 Samuel Smithson
1807 John D.Dixon
1808 William Leach
1815 William Wood
1819 John Walker
1820 Stephen Fawcett
1824 T. Parker
1825 S. Hearfield
1838 Thomas Fox
1841 Stephen Fawcett

Until 1843 the wardens would have been called Chapelwardens. They are called Churchwardens in the press report of the consecration of St. Mary's in that year.
The list of wardens up to 1860 is based on a list in Rev Charles Ingham Black's book, *Historical Memoirals of Burley by the Wharfe* and verified as far as possible by the Chapel Wardens' Accounts, recorded in *Burley Town Book* up to 1814. After that the names are recorded in the *Vestry Minute Book* up to 1920.
The custom of having two wardens seems to have begun in 1850. The naming of one as Vicar's Warden (V) and People's Warden (P) was not begun until 1867.

1842	Joseph Whitehead	
1845	W. Hearfield	
1847	Charles Whitaker	
1848	John Lupton	
1849	John W. Scriven	
1850	John W. Scriven	J. Wood
1851	T. Pawson	H. Smith
1852	T. Swain	J. Fox
1853	William Fison	T. Taylor
1854	W. Hargreaves	E. Brumfitt
1855	W. Hargreaves	G. Holmes
1856	T. Taylor	W. Swain
1857	T. Taylor	J. Towers
1858	T. Taylor	W. Swain
1859	William Fison	E. H. Hudson
1860	Thomas Clark	J. Whitworth
1861	T. Taylor	J. Whitworth
1864	Horner Harrison	J. Whitworth
1866	Horner Harrison	Frederick W. Fox
1867	Robert Hudson (V)	Frederick W. Fox (P)
1869	Robert Hudson (V)	Robert Fox (P)
1873	John Rouse (V)	Robert Fox (P)
1874	Edward P. Arnold (V)	Robert Fox (P)
1877	W. H. Job (V)	Robert Fox (P)
1878	John Lupton (V)	Robert Fox (P)
1884	Walter Bairstow (V)	Robert Fox (P)
1889	W. H. Jenkins (V)	Robert Fox (P)
1891	Dr. H. Hebblethwaite (V)	Robert Fox (P)
1893	James Stradling (V)	Robert Fox (P)
1894	Reginald S. Yorke (V)	Robert Fox (P)
1896	W. H. Mitchell (V)	Robert Fox (P)
1898	? Westerman (V)	Robert Fox (P)
1900	Thomas Butterfield (V)	Robert Fox (P)
1902	George Wood (V)	Robert Fox (P)
1903	Arthur Greenwood (V)	Robert Fox (P)

1909	Arthur Greenwood (V)	John Exley (P)
1910	Edward P. Arnold-Forster (V)	John Exley (P)
1913	Frederick D. Moore (V)	John Exley (P)
1919	John Exley (V)	Fred Vine (P)
1925	E.G.H. Mitchell (V)	Fred Vine (P)
1931	H. Chorley (V)	Fred Vine (P)
1932	H. Chorley (V)	Fred Vine (died in office)
		F. Midgley (P)
1935	H. Chorley (V)	William Newbould (P)
1937	Dr. J. Garscadden (V)	William Newbould (P)
1939	Dr. J. Garscadden (V)	William Newbould (died in office
		Herman Weightman (P)
1940	T.A. Mallinson (V)	Herman Weightman (P)
1945	T.A. Mallinson (V)	F.A. Walker (P)
1946	James V. Slater (V)	F.A. Walker (P)
1950	James V. Slater (V)	John Rayner (P)
1952	James V. Slater (V)	F.W.B. (Eric) Maufe (P)
1966	James V. Slater (V)	Moses (Sam) Wheeler (P)
1972	James V. Slater (V)	W. (Pip) Hayes (P)
1973	Harry Hornby (V)	Pip Hayes (P)

The distinction between Vicar's (V) and People's (P) Warden seems to have been dropped. It is not mentioned in the Minutes after this date.

1981	Rex Madin	Pip Hayes
1985	Rex Madin	Ian Walsh
1986	Frank Schofield	Ian Walsh
1992	Keith Dale	Ian Walsh
1994	Keith Dale	Paul Evans (Assistant Warden,
		Irene Exley)
1998	Mark Selby	Paul Evans
2001	Mark Selby	Duncan Watts
2004	Janet Squire	Duncan Watts
2005	Janet Squire	Gail Boole

APPENDIX FOUR
ARTICLE IN *CHURCH TIMES* 15TH MAY 2009

A Question of Sharing.
Why can't money be shared more?
Dennis Warwick

The columns of *The Church Times* frequently address the subject of Parish Shares. A scan of archived comments over the last five years or so gives an idea of the issues which are raised. Parish Shares set by Dioceses, to cover their costs including the stipends and pensions of clergy, inevitably cause PCCs and regular givers serious bouts of indigestion. One commentator from a parish (said to be one of the most affluent) in Berkshire last year noted the shock horror at the annual meeting when it was announced that the Share had gone up in one year from £60,000 to £90,000. Some parishes are serial defaulters, adding to the Share burden of other parishes in their Diocese. Others worry that the increase in Parish Shares is diverting money which could be going to charities and overseas support. Diocesan administrators wryly point to the increasing difficulty they have in balancing the books. The 'credit crunch' is currently not making life any easier for them nor for the Church Commissioners in meeting the needs of the Church of England.

I write this article from a relatively affluent parish in the Diocese of Bradford. For the first time in many years our PCC, of which I am a member, has opted reluctantly to default on its Parish Share. Our total income from every source in 2008 was £163,103 of which £27,845 is restricted. The Diocese has requested us to pay £126,300 in 2009, but we would not have enough left to pay for all our other immediate mission commitments in the parish if we paid our Share in full. Further we are concerned that the requested Share is taking an increasing proportion of our income. Over the past fifty years our Parish Share as a percentage of annual church income has risen from 14.6 in 1960, to 50.0 in 1983, to 59.3 in 2003 and to 77.4 in 2009 (or to 92.0 if we deduct restricted funds from our income).

We are not alone in this situation. Other parishes in a similar geographical and economic situation in our Diocese are faced with large requests. In its summary of 'The Share System' in November 2008, the Bradford Diocesan Board of Finance noted that 'some Dioceses have substantial reserves or local trusts which provide significant income for various areas of expenditure which in Bradford need to be funded through Share. As a result of lack of such funds and the relatively small number of parishes in the Diocese, it is acknowledged as a fact that Share is higher per member than in most other Dioceses'. In another recent paper on 'The Future of the Bradford Diocese' presented to the Diocesan Synod in February 2009, it was noted that 'our parish shares are comparatively high but so are our giving levels'.

This situation prompted me to find out what is the situation in other Dioceses. Some Diocesan websites provide information about Parish Shares but generally the data is very sketchy. In consequence I have undertaken a survey by contacting friends or friends of friends across the country in the last two months to look at the distribution of Parish Shares. The ensuing table attempts to draw comparisons between the parish shares in other Dioceses. The parishes are not named but an indication of the character of the parish is given in the comments column. The interesting column which shows the contrasts most clearly is that where an attempt is made to assess the amount of Share per giver. In the parishes where the number of active regular givers is known, this seems to be roughly two thirds of the number on the Electoral Roll. I have used 65 percent somewhat arbitrarily as the multiplying factor. The column 'Share per Giver' is computed by dividing the parish share by 65 percent of the number on the electoral roll.

Many criticisms can be levelled at this presentation. It is in no way a scientifically drawn sample. There are 43 Dioceses in England and they vary tremendously in the historical, social and economic factors which will determine how much each Diocese requests of its parishes. Not all the parishes have a similar social composition or parish population. I have sent emails to a number of Diocesan Boards of Finance asking what their highest Parish Share is, but only one replied, giving a figure that was slightly less than that in my parish. Generally however the information suggests that the Director of the Board of Finance for Bradford Diocese is correct in noting the inequity that exists among Dioceses. On a local level, the principle of richer parishes supporting poorer parishes is one to which we are committed. We believe that mutual support is essential, the strong carry the weak, and the rich help the poor. On a national level we note however that there seems to be a reluctance to apply the principle to Dioceses.

Diocese	Electoral Roll	Parish Share £	Parish Share per giver £. p	Comments on the Parish
Chichester	138	57,180	637.46	Village church, 1 Vicar, affluent area
Canterbury	204	61,409	463.11	Small coastal town, 1 Vicar
Norwich	210	72,000	527.47	Small town, 1 Vicar, relative affluent
Oxford 1	148	47,872	497.63	Mixed rural, commuters, 1 Vicar
Oxford 2	250	45,300	278.77	3 Affluent villages, 1 Vicar
Worcester	183	93,000	572.31	Market town, 1 Vicar and 1 Curate
Derby	175	55,000	483.52	Relatively affluent suburb, 2 Priests
Chester	117	48,120	632.74	Affluent commuter village, 1 Vicar
Manchester	240	49,237	315.62	Urban Parish, 5 churches, 1 Vicar
Durham	274	52,779	296.34	Market town Parish, average wealth
Carlisle	132	41,480	483.45	Former industrial parish, p/t Vicar
Blackburn	150	60,000	615.38	Market town, average wealth,1 Vicar
Ripon/Leeds	177	82,144	713.99	Relatively affluent suburb, 1 Vicar
Bradford	240	126,300	809.62	Affluent village, 1 Vicar, 1/2 Curate

Table 2. Variation in Parish Shares across a number of Dioceses.

Twenty six years ago the then Archbishop of Canterbury, Robert Runcie, set up a commission to look into what the Church was doing about the urban poor in this country. The ensuing report, *Faith in the City*, published in 1985, caused a huge stir. It identified the huge inequalities in incomes, life chances, education and family life existing in Britain at that time. Surveys carried out recently show that while some amelioration has occurred there are still many social inequalities. On the question of what the Church should do in 1985, *Faith in the City* asked the Church to strengthen its presence in the Urban Priority Areas. It noted however that the existing framework of financial support was not equitable. There were big differences in the resources which some Dioceses could command compared with others. 'Dioceses, as well as parish Churches, must be outward looking: they should not seek to rest comfortably on a financial cushion provided by the generosity of past Christians or by the vagaries of history and population movements' the report suggested. Parishes within a Diocese should work in partnership and Dioceses too should seek to iron out inequalities between them.

It is very difficult of course to find out what historical resources Dioceses have. Most of the 43 do not publish detailed financial statements on their web sites. They play their cards close to their chests, particularly since the Church Commissioners have thrown much of the cost of maintaining clergy pensions largely back to the Dioceses. The Dioceses must finance these from their resources and from the Parish Share. According to a reliable informant who has served for many years on a Diocesan Synod and at one time on the Bishop's Council in that Diocese, the Church Commissioners used in the 1960s to support Dioceses up to 80% of their needs, whereas now it is no more than 20%. The Church of England website (www.cofe.anglican.org) says that the Commissioners contribute about 18% at present. There is some discriminatory support for those Dioceses which have needy parishes, and Bradford Diocese does receive extra financial help for that reason.

The *Financial Times* published on 12th July 2008 an article in its Weekend Magazine, (Richard Tomkins, 'A religion in recession') purporting to give a financial portrait of the Church of England. It stressed shrinking congregations, soaring costs, and crumbling buildings. Nevertheless the article noted that 'the Church Commissioners' land, property and stock market investments were valued at £5.7 billions at the last balance sheet date and last year (2007) contributed £177.8 millions to the Church of England revenues'. The resources held by the Dioceses themselves include land, possibly as much as 129,000 acres, and historic buildings, such as bishop's palaces, churches, parsonages, church halls, graveyards and glebe land. Many will be producing rents and many others have been sold off as parishes have merged and incumbents have been rehoused in more modern accommodation. All this, the article concludes, contributes about a quarter to the Church's annual spending needs. Much of the rest is coming from the parishioners, and they of course are a declining number. Other income comes from weddings and funerals, special fund-raising and some trading activities. The basic fact remains that some Dioceses are much better placed financially than others to meet their running costs just as *Faith in the City* indicated nearly 25 years ago.

What then should be done? Crucially there should be a thorough and transparent review of the resources available to the Church of England and its Dioceses along with some forecasts of future trends and ways in which the Church might respond. The new Dioceses Commission which was set up in 2008 has a primary duty to keep under review the provincial and diocesan structure of the Church of England and in particular:

the size, boundaries and number of provinces;
the size, boundaries and number of dioceses and their distribution between the provinces;
the number and distribution of bishops and the arrangements for episcopal oversight.

It will be of no permanent value, however, if the Dioceses Commission just looks at administrative structures. Clearly these have financial implications. Surely the crucial dimension is in equalizing the wealth of Dioceses. It is not right that some parishes in relatively poor Dioceses should have to bear their present inequitable burdens.

54. St. Mary's BV Church: spire and west end, 2006.

REFERENCES

1. Rev. R. V. Taylor, *Ecclesiae Leodienses or Architectural Sketches of the Churches of Leeds and Neighbourhood,* Roland Jackson, Leeds, 1875, p. 232.
2. Rev. C.I. Black, *Some Short Historical Memorials of the Ancient Chapelry of Burley-by-the-Wharfe and Mensington or Menston,* 1868.
3. Taylor, op. cit. p. 23.
4. Rt. Rev. C.T. Longley, Bishop of Ripon, *Notebooks of Visitation 1830-1856: Burley P.C.* Holden Library, Special Collections, Brotherton Library, University of Leeds.
5. *Leeds Intelligencer,* 24th June 1843, *The Consecration of St. Mary's Church, Burley-in-Wharfedale* (See Appendix Two).
6. Burley's *Town Book,* 1763-1814, West Yorkshire Archives Service, Bradford Central Library.
7. John Peele Clapham was a lawyer and a staunch Independent churchman known to have had experience of Sunday School work in Leeds. *The Annals of a Village Sunday School,* an anonymous unpaginated publication of 1874, possibly by Clapham, gives a full account of the difficulties and negotiations between Clapham and Hodgkinson in 1835. *The Annals* were made available to us by John Breare of Skipton (now deceased) a former resident of Burley and an officer of Salem United Reformed Church, founded in Burley by Clapham in 1840.
8. *The Annals of a Village Sunday School.*
9. Ibid.
10. Ibid.
11. Longley, op.cit.
12. It was the same Wilkinson who seems to have been the instrument in the ending of the ecumenical school founded by agreement between John Peele Clapham and Edmund Hodgkinson, and setting in train the institution of a National School in Burley.
13. *Report to the General Board of Health on the Sanitary Condition of the Inhabitants of the Township of Burley in the parish of Otley,* by William Ranger, Superintending Inspector, February 15th 1854. Copy in Bradford Central Library. The ensuing developments in local government have been described in M. & D. Warwick, *Independent Burley: A Village, its People and its Councils,* Burley Local History Group, 2006.
14. Frances Knight, *The Nineteenth Century Church and English Society,* Cambridge University Press, 1995. p. 1.

15. Ibid.

16. In 1851, in addition to the census of population a census was taken of attendance places of worship. Although this was purely voluntary, most places of worship made returns. The returns for England and Wales are now among the Home Office Records in National Archives (HO 129). Clergy completing the returns were asked to discover 'how far the means of Religious Instruction provided in Great Britain during the last fifty years have kept pace with the population during the same period, and to what extent those means are adequate to meet the spiritual wants of the increased population of 1851'. A total of 34,467 forms were returned for England and Wales. Of these, 2524 contained no information about sittings, 1394 contained no information about church attendance and 390 returned forms had no information on either sittings or attendance. The returns show the name and denomination of each place of worship, including those of Roman Catholic and dissenting Protestant congregations, the date of consecration or erection of the building and the space available for public worship. They usually give totals of attendances at the various services on 30th March 1851, and average attendances for the previous year. They often include information about buildings and endowments and comments by the Minister.

17. There was much criticism of the whole exercise of having a religious census. It was never again repeated.

18. These details are taken from *Crockford's Clerical Directory of 1880*, H. Speight, *Upper Wharfedale*, Elliot Stock, 1900 and *The Gentleman's Magazine*, July 1855.

19. The specification for the vicarage can be found in West Yorkshire Archives, Bradford Central Library, Ref BDP/33 dated 1853.

20. The Census Enumerators' Books for Burley Township are: for 1861, RG/9/3213; 1871, RG/10/4302; 1881, RG/11/4336; 1891, RG/12/3527.

21. *Memorials* op. cit. *Pastoral Address*, dated Advent 1855.

22. Ibid. Advent 1856.

23. Frances Knight, op. cit. p. 5.

24. *A financial and statistical review of clerical life for eighteen years*: A letter to F.W. Fox, Whitsuntide 1873, included in the collection of printed papers in *Historical Memorials*.

25. Ibid.

26. H. Speight, op.cit. p. 145.

27. A letter (formerly in the archives of St. Mary's) from Greeholme Mills

dated January 30th 1867 from W.E. Forster to Robert Fox, one of the Churchwardens, indicates some of the discussions which were going on before the alterations: ' Dear Sir, As I leave home for London this week, I write a line that I now think it will be better for the reseating the body of the church to be done at the same time as any alterations are made in the building—I would therefore suggest to the committee that when a church architect has been fixed upon to superintend the alterations in the building, he be requested to give plan and estimate for reseating and warming and lighting the body of the church—Upon such plan being approved by the Committee I shall be glad to see it. I may mention that the views from many persons are that the reseating of Ilkley Church has been done well. Yours truly.....'

28. The faculty and associated documents are held in the Ripon Diocesan papers, Leeds Archives at Sheepscar, reference RD/AF2/4/2.

29. Frances Knight, op.cit. pp 60—71.

30. The Journals of Frances Egerton Arnold-Forster, Vol. 2, pp. 110-114, Brotherton Library Special Collections, University of Leeds. Frances was one of the four adopted children of William and Jane Forster. Jane was the daughter of Thomas Arnold of Rugby. Her brother William Arnold and his wife both died in the late 1850s leaving four children orphaned. The Forsters adopted them and brought them up in Burley at Wharfeside. As William became M.P. for Bradford soon after they were adopted, they did not spend all their young lives in Burley, but whenever they were in the Village, they were regular attenders at St. Mary's. Frances in her Journals refers to church life in Burley. When they all reached their maturity they changed their surnames from Arnold to Arnold-Forster in gratitude to their foster-parents. For further information see M. & D. Warwick, *Eminent Victorians: The Forsters of Burley-in-Wharfedale,* Burley Local History Group, 1994.

31. A written note attached to the *Vestry Book*, Burley Parish Records, West Yorkshire Archives, Bradford Central Library, BDP/33/2/1/1.

32. From a printed letter to parishioners attached to the Register of Services, 1878, ibid. BDP33/2/1.

33. Letter to F.W. Fox, *Historical Memorials* op. cit.

34. Registers of Services, op. cit. 1873.

35. Until 1950 the Church School in the Village was known as the National School. When the School was founded in 1837, it was registered with the National Society. This Society was founded by Andrew Bell in 1811 as the

National Society for the Education of the Poor in the Doctrine and Discipline of the Established Church. The Society gave grants to its registered schools.

36.   This section on the National School is an edited version of Chapter Three in M. & D. Warwick, *Our Schools: A History of Schools in Burley-in-Wharfedale*, Burley Local History Group, 1998, pp 18—33.

37.   The book of poems *Memorialia Cordis* published in London and Dublin in 1856 contains several which show how he was inspired by the natural world and religious themes. There are love poems no doubt reflecting his recent marriage, or possibly even earlier romances. His Irish heritage is also clearly reflected as are thoughts on significant events of the past. The book of poems is still available on line through Google. *The Proselytes of Ishmael: Being a short Historical Survey of the Turanian Tribes in their Western Migrations,* published in London in 1879 is also available in second hand book shops and is advertised on line.

38.   "Pneumatomachy" is the name for a heresy, first noted in the 4th Century, in a sect which denied the divinity or personality of the Holy Spirit.

39.   *The Real Presence of God the Holy Ghost* reprinted with additions from the *Church Review*, London, The Church Press Company Ltd, 1866, is a ten page pamphlet bound into *Historical Memorials*. It was a sermon given to fellow priests at a Eucharist on St. Mark's Day, 1866.

40.   *The Deadly Sin: a letter to the Women of the West Riding,* a pamphlet printed by the Church Press Company of London, 1868 is bound into *Historical Memorials.* It had a long print run and is introduced as the *Third Thousand*, suggesting it had a wide circulation.

41.   *Lyra Eucharistica:hymns and verses on the Holy Communion, Ancient and Modern*, edited by Rev Orby Shipley, Longman Green, 1864 is available on line at http://www.archive,org/stream/lyraeucharistica.

42.   Dr. Black's carol, *T'was in the winter cold*, was published in the influential book entitled *Christmas Carols New and Old*, 1871. It was compiled by Rev H.R. Bramley, Fellow of Magdalen College, Oxford and Dr. John Stainer, then organist of the College. The influence of this book was enormous as it placed in the hands of the clergy a really practicable tool, which was in general use for nearly 60 years. It is mainly to Bramley and Stainer that we owe the restoration of the carol, according to Percy Dearmer, the editor of the first *Oxford Book of Carols* in 1928. Black's carol can be accessed online at http://www.cyberhymnal.org/htm/t/i/w/tiwincold.htm

43.   The British and Foreign Schools Society was set up in 1808 by Joseph

Lancaster as a non-denominational body, providing stimulus for the training of teachers. He was a Quaker who became concerned that the poorer classes were denied the opportunity of education. The Lancastrian system (on monitorial system) used older children who had already been given some instruction to teach younger ones. It was designed to provide a cheap basic education with limited resources and a limited number of teachers.

44.   Florence O'Brien, nee Arnold-Forster, kept a diary, extracts of which have been kindly made available to us by Veronica Rowe, her granddaughter, and David her husband of County Dublin.

45.   The education dispute is dealt with at length in Chapter 4 of M & D Warwick, op. cit. 1998.

46.   John Lupton kept a foolscap size diary which fortunately was rescued from the bin by Ann Smith, wife of Harry 'Gas' Smith of Spring Gardens some 25 years ago. Harry was one of John Lupton's descendants. Unfortunately only fragments of the diary remain and those are for the years 1900, 1903 and 1905, but they are sufficient to give us a very real impression of one of who worshipped at St. Mary's for many years in both Black's and Stedman's time.

47.   *Independent Burley: A Village, its People and its Councils*, 2006, p.33. Foulds, a councillor who had served Burley Local Board and the Urban District Council for 50 years, spoke about meetings being held in 'Old Parish Rooms, before the purchase of the Grange as Council offices.

48.   Article in *Ilkley Free Press*, dated 7th September 1900.

49.   Ibid. 4th January 1901.

50.   See endnote 44.

51.   The Bradford centre for the West Yorkshire Archives in Bradford Central Library contains among the Parish Records, a number of Parish Magazines (ref. BDP33/12/1-6). All the issues for 1903 though decaying rapidly are in the Archives, but there are only sample issues for the rest of the 20th Century.

52.   Rt. Rev. Frederick Temple born 1821 died 1902, was an ordained master at Rugby School, spent some time in Whitehall in the Education Department, was made Bishop of Exeter in 1869, Bishop of London in 1885 and Archbishop of Canterbury in 1896. He was the father of William Temple, later Archbishop of York and then Canterbury.

53.   The plans for this proposed Church are in the Bradford Central Library, West Yorkshire Archives section, BDP33/5/6/1.

54. Details of the formation of the new Diocese of Bradford can be found in Astrid Hansen, *One Small Corner, A History of Bradford Diocese,* Bradford Diocesan Board of Finance, 1994.

55. Roger Lloyd, *The Church of England, 1900-1965*, SCM Press, 1966, p. 349.

56. *Wharfedale and Airedale Observer*, 27th February 1937.

57. *Ilkley Gazette,* 12th August 1938.

58. PCC minutes, 1942-1943.

59. *General Rubricks of the Administration of the Lord's Supper or Holy Communion,* Book of Common Prayer, 1662 revision.

60. PCC minutes of the Annual Meeting, March 1945.

61. William Temple, *Christianity and Social Order,* 1942, quoted in Canon A.E. Baker, *William Temple and his Message*, Penguin Books, 1946.

62. PCC Minutes 1945.

63. Astrid Hansen, op. cit. p. 86.

64. PCC Minutes 1954.

65. At this time Chaplains to hospitals received a small salary from the National Health Service budget.

66. Kelham College was set up by the Society of the Sacred Mission in 1890 to train candidates for the ministry who would be drawn from all social classes. The Society recognized that the cost of university education followed by theological training prohibited all but the wealthy upper and middle classes of Victorian England from realising a vocation to the priesthood. This continued to be its aim until the 1970s when the College closed as the number of candidates for ordination dwindled. In some ways it was similar to the Community of the Resurrection in Mirfield, which was primarily a religious community, but which sent young men to Leeds University to read for a degree followed by theological training for the ministry. Kelham provided its own courses for those who could profess a real vocation but who had not advanced beyond secondary education. Candidates could enter at 15 or 16 years and undergo a course of up to seven years in length in the Classics, History, Theology and Philosophy, before ordination. During the second World War, the College was taken over by the Armed Forces, which is possibly where John Beardsmore first came into contact with it. He returned there for his training in 1946.

67. The Vicar speaking at the Annual Vestry and Parochial meeting, 1957.

68. Christian Stewardship Progress Report, The Parish Church of St. Mary BV, Burley-in-Wharfedale, February 1963.

69. Ibid.
70. Archbishop Ramsey, 1961, quoted in Paul A. Welsby, *A History of the Church of England,* 1945-1980, Oxford University Press, 1984 p. 158.
71. Letter of 7th January 1969, addressed to Jim Bennett, Secretary of the PCC, from Henry Firth, Registrar and Secretary to the Lord Bishop of Bradford.
72. Letter from the Secretary of the PCC to the Diocesan Registrar, 29th January 1969.
73. Astrid Hansen, op.cit. p.134.
74. Extracts from 'The Consideration' in Burley-in-Wharfedale, April 1970.
75. Diocese of Bradford, A Summary of the Parochial Reports on 'The Consideration', 1970, p.3.
76. Paul A. Welsby, op.cit. p.211.
77. The Village Fete now held on the first Saturday in July each year has more recently been organised by Parent Teacher Associations and not the Churches.
78. We are indebted for this story to Michael Hardstaffe a Lay Preacher of Burley Methodist Church.
79. Audrey Birch reporting to the Annual Parochial Church meeting, February 1974.
80. *The Yorkshire Post,* 3rd December 1976.
81. The ten favourite hymns in order from the most popular: *The Lord's my Shepherd; The Day Thou gavest; Praise My Soul; Onward Christian Soldiers; O Jesus I have promised; Lord Jesus Christ You have come to us; I danced in the morning; Guide me O my great Redeemer; Dear Lord and Father of mankind; and Abide with me.*
82. *Paul A. Welsby,* op. cit. p. 240.
83. Lois Fulker some twenty years later was able to take an ordination course at Durham University and became a Deacon and a Priest in the Diocese of Carlisle.
84. *Ilkley Gazette,* 13th January 1994.
85. Report of the Archbishop of Canterbury's Commission on Urban Priority Areas, *Faith in the City, A Call for Action by Church and Nation,* Church House Publishing, London, 1985.
86. 'Forward together in Faith, Christian Stewardship Mission', 1989, Rev. Peter Burwell, Diocesan Stewardship Adviser. A duplicated report.
87. 'Ichthus' is a Greek word, meaning 'Fish' and the fish was a secret symbol used by early Christians to signify membership of what was a proscribed

sect. The association of fish with Christianity is fairly obvious in that several of the disciples were fishermen, and fish feature significantly in the miracle of the feeding of the five thousand.

88.   'A Woman's Place in the Church', *Wharfedale and Airedale Observer,* 31st March 1989.

89.   Bradford Council created a Conservation Area in the middle of Burley in the 1980s which covered the buildings and layout of the village along Main Street and parcels of land several metres on either side of it. The idea of the Conservation Area was to maintain the character of the village and prevent development out of sympathy with it. St. Mary's Church lies within the Conservation Area.

90.   'Half a Century Celebrated', article in the *Wharfedale and Airedale Observer*, 8th October 1992.

91.   Donald Aldred died in July 1993 while still Rector of Holy Trinity Church Skipton. His wife Janet had died after a long struggle with cancer in 1990.

92.   'Churches Together in Burley and Menston' was formed in 1994 when it was realised that Burley Christian Council was not ecumenical enough, for it nominally excluded Menston members of the Catholic Community of Saints John Fisher and Thomas More. Also the general ecumenical mood of the time was leading people to name the groups 'Churches Together'.

93.   Judy Taylor, 'Report on the Open Door', published in the Annual Report of the Parish Church, 13th April 1997.

94.   David Jenkins, *The Calling of a Cuckoo, Not Quite an Autobiography*, pp 149-151, Continuum, London 2002.

95.   From the preface to *Common Worship*, p. ix Church House Publishing, London, 2000.

96.   Christingle services had been introduced at St. Mary's in the early 1970s by Janet Aldred.

97.   The mission statement emerged from a series of Way Ahead workshops and was adopted as a Statement of Purpose by the PCC in July 2000. It has been slightly amended from the original.

98.   Extract from the speech of the Bishop of Guildford to the House of Lords, 30th March 2001.

99.   David Jenkins, op.cit. p.171.

BIBLIOGRAPHY

PRIMARY SOURCES

Charles Ingham Black, *Some Short Historical Memorials of the Ancient Chapelry of Burley-by-the-Wharfe and Mensington or Menston*, 1868? Copy in St. Mary's Parish Archives.

Burley's *Town Book*, 1763-1814, West Yorkshire Archives Service, Bradford Central Library.

The Annals of a Village Sunday School, an anonymous publication, possibly by John Peele Clapham, 1874. Copy made available to us by J. Breare, in Burley Village Archives, Burley Public Library.

Faculty for the replacement of the old Chapel and construction of the new building in 1843, York Diocesan Records at the Borthwick Institute, University of York.

Rt. Rev C.T. Longley, Bishop of Ripon, *Notebooks of Visitation 1830-1856: Burley P.C.,* Holden Library, Special Collections, Brotherton Library, University of Leeds. Bishop Longley records seven visitations between 1837 and 1856.

Vestry Book, Burley Parish Records, West Yorkshire Archives, Bradford Central Library, ref. BDP/33/2/1/1.

Faculty and Correspondence related to the Church Extension, 1869, Ripon Diocesan papers, Leeds Archives at Sheepscar, reference RD/AF2/4/2.

The Journals of Frances Egerton Arnold-Forster, 1871-1887, Brotherton Library Special Collections, University of Leeds.

John Lupton, 'A Diary' (surviving photocopied extracts for 1900, 1903 and 1905), Burley Village Archives, Burley Public Library.

Census of Places of Religious Worship, 1851, The National Archives, HO129.

Minutes of the St. Mary's Parochial Church Council and Annual Vestry and Parochial Meetings, from 1920, Burley Parish Records, West Yorkshire Archives, Bradford Central Library, BDP33/13/4/2.

A number of Parish Magazines and other papers published by the Church can also be consulted in the West Yorkshire Archives, Bradford Central Library, ref. BDP33/12.

SECONDARY SOURCES.

Archbishop of Canterbury's Commission on Urban Priority Areas, Report: *Faith in the City: A Call for Action by Church and Nation*, Church House Publishing, London, 1985.

Canon A.E. Baker, *William Temple and his Message*, Penguin Books, London, 1946.

Crockford's Clerical Directory, Church House Publishing, London. (First edition, 1858).

David Jenkins, *The Calling of a Cuckoo, Not Quite an Autobiography*, Continuum, London 2002.

Frances Knight, *The Nineteenth Century Church and English Society*, Cambridge University Press, 1995.

Frances Knight, *The Church in the Nineteenth Century*, Tauris, London, 2008

Roger Lloyd, *The Church of England, 1900-1965*, SCM Press, 1966.

David Nealy, *The Parish Church of Burley-in-Wharfedale*, W. Walker, Otley, 1960.

Frank Newbould, *A Short History of the Parish Church of St. Mary the Blessed Virgin*, Typed and Duplicated for the Church's 150th Anniversary, 1993.

H. Speight, *Upper Wharfedale*, Elliot Stock, 1900.

Rev. R. V. Taylor, *Ecclesiae Leodienses or Architectural Sketches of the Churches of Leeds and Neighbourhood*, Roland Jackson, Leeds, 1875.

M. & D. Warwick, *Independent Burley: A Village, its People and its Councils,* Burley Local History Group, 2006.

M. & D. Warwick, *Our Schools: A History of Schools in Burley-in-Wharfedale,* Burley Local History Group, 1998.

Paul A. Welsby, *A History of the Church of England,* 1945-1980, Oxford University Press, 1984.

B. G. Worrall, *The Making of the Modern Church: Christianity in England since 1800,* Third Edition, S.PC.K. London, 2004.

NEWSPAPERS:

Leeds Intelligencer, 1843.

Ilkley Free Press.

Ilkley Gazette.

Wharfedale and Airedale Observer.

Wharfedale Pictorial.

Yorkshire Post.

A Prayer.

Rev. Michael Burley

Our Father, we thank you:
For the witness of St. Mary's church.
For the many people who have been part of the community
here.
For the lives we have touched with the good news of Jesus.
For the people we have served in His name.
For each opportunity we have had to show love.
We pray you would continue to bless our mission now and
always,
that your Son, our Lord Jesus Christ may be worshipped,
praised and adored,
and that His Kingdom may come in glory.
Amen.